# Table of Contents

The Need for Spiritual Detox ..................................................... 5

Understanding Your Spiritual Energy ..................................... 23

Releasing Negative Attachments ............................................. 47

Cleansing the Mind for Spiritual Clarity ................................. 69

Emotional Healing and Spiritual Renewal ............................. 89

Detoxing Your Environment for Spiritual Growth .............. 107

Aligning with Your True Self .................................................. 125

Building Spiritual Resilience .................................................. 141

Sustaining Your Spiritual Detox Long-Term ....................... 157

A New Beginning ..................................................................... 175

# The Need for Spiritual Detox

*"Cleanse your spirit, and you will hear the whispers of your true self beneath the noise of the world."*

## Defining Spiritual Detox

Spiritual detox is the process of removing internal blockages, negative energy, and limiting beliefs that accumulate over time. Just as the body can be burdened by toxins from food, the environment, or unhealthy habits, the mind and soul can also become weighed down by negativity, unresolved emotions, and outdated thought patterns. These internal obstructions create a sense of heaviness, preventing clarity, inner peace, and a deeper spiritual connection.

At its core, spiritual detox is about clearing space—mentally, emotionally, and energetically. By letting go of what no longer serves us, we make room for self-awareness, renewal, and alignment with our true selves. This process is not about adopting a new belief system or following strict rules but rather about stripping away the layers of interference that keep us from experiencing a pure, unfiltered connection with our own consciousness and the world around us.

Throughout life, experiences, societal conditioning, and personal struggles contribute to the buildup of emotional and spiritual residue. This can manifest as recurring negative thoughts, chronic stress, self-doubt, or a sense of disconnection from one's purpose. Spiritual detox is a way to address these blockages, providing an opportunity to reset and realign with inner harmony.

The journey of spiritual detox is deeply personal. Some may find renewal through meditation, breathwork, journaling, or solitude, while others turn to energy healing, nature, or intentional self-reflection. Regardless of the method, the goal remains the same: to release the burdens that cloud the spirit and create space for peace, clarity, and deeper connection.

**Why Detox the Soul?**

Just as a cluttered space can feel overwhelming, a cluttered soul can create chaos within. Spiritual clutter—accumulated negative thoughts, unresolved trauma, and energy imbalances—acts as an invisible weight, influencing emotions, thoughts, and even physical health. Over time, these burdens drain vitality, disrupt mental clarity, and create emotional distress, leading to feelings of stagnation, disconnection, or even unexplained exhaustion.

Negative thoughts, especially when repeated, shape perception and behavior. The mind is incredibly powerful, and its patterns dictate the way we experience life. When negativity takes root, it can become a self-perpetuating cycle, reinforcing beliefs of unworthiness, fear, or failure. These thoughts, when left unchecked, influence the way we interact with the world, limiting potential and keeping us stuck in a state of mental and emotional exhaustion. Self-doubt, for example, can create an internal resistance to change or growth, while fear and guilt may hold us back from pursuing opportunities or healing past wounds. The longer these patterns persist, the more deeply they become ingrained, making it difficult to break free.

Trauma, whether acknowledged or suppressed, stores itself in the body and mind, subtly influencing reactions, relationships, and overall well-being. Past emotional wounds, even those we think we have moved on from, can continue to affect our daily lives. The subconscious mind holds onto painful memories, replaying them in different situations, sometimes without us even realizing it. This can result in emotional triggers, patterns of avoidance, or difficulty forming deep and meaningful connections with others. Spiritual detox allows for the recognition and release of these stored emotions, bringing them to the surface so they can be processed and healed. Without this release, trauma continues to manifest in various ways—through chronic stress, anxiety, or even physical ailments.

Energy imbalances, often result from stress or exposure to toxic environments, manifest as irritability, anxiety, or persistent fatigue. Everything in life carries energy, from the people we interact with to the environments we spend time in. When we are constantly surrounded by negativity, conflict, or overwhelming demands, our energy field absorbs these influences, creating a state of imbalance. Over time, this leads to a persistent sense of depletion, where even small tasks feel exhausting. This kind of imbalance can also create emotional instability, leading to heightened sensitivity, mood swings, or a constant feeling of being on edge. A spiritual detox serves as a reset, helping to clear away external influences and restore balance to our internal state.

The connection between spiritual detox and overall wellness is profound. Emotionally, clearing internal blockages allows for greater resilience, balance, and a sense of peace. Mental well-being is deeply intertwined with emotional health—when the mind is burdened with negativity, it struggles to maintain focus, creativity, and a sense of purpose. Without a regular detox, the mind can become cluttered with intrusive thoughts, worry, and over analysis, leading to stress and burnout. Mentally, spiritual detox fosters clarity, reducing overthinking and self-sabotaging thought patterns. When the mind is free from excessive mental chatter, it becomes easier to see solutions, make decisions with confidence, and cultivate a sense of inner peace.

Physically, unresolved energy imbalances can contribute to tension, headaches, digestive issues, or weakened immunity—signals that deeper healing is needed. The body and mind are intricately connected, meaning that internal distress often manifests in physical symptoms. Stress, for example, can trigger chronic inflammation, disrupt sleep patterns, and weaken the immune system, making us more susceptible to illness. Unresolved emotions, particularly those tied to past trauma, may create muscle tension, unexplained pain, or even long-term conditions that doctors struggle to diagnose. When we detox spiritually, we allow the body to return to a state of harmony, reducing stress-related ailments and promoting overall well-being.

By detoxing the soul, we create space for renewal, joy, and authentic self-expression. The process of letting go is not just about removing negativity—it is also about inviting in new energy, fresh perspectives, and a sense of lightness. When we release what no longer serves us, we restore harmony within ourselves, making room for growth, creativity, and a deeper connection to both ourselves and the world. True fulfillment comes not from external achievements but from inner peace, and a spiritual detox is the key to accessing that state of being.

**Signs You Need a Spiritual Detox**

The signs that a spiritual detox is needed often appear gradually, manifesting as emotional, mental, and even physical symptoms. Just as the body signals when it needs rest and nourishment, the soul also communicates when it is overwhelmed with spiritual clutter. These signals are easy to overlook in the busyness of everyday life, but when left unaddressed, they can accumulate, creating feelings of stagnation, exhaustion, and disconnection. Recognizing these warning signs is the first step toward clearing internal blockages and restoring balance.

One of the most telling indicators that a spiritual detox is necessary is chronic stress. While stress is a natural response to certain life challenges, ongoing and unrelenting stress—even in situations that don't warrant it—suggests a deeper internal imbalance. This kind of stress often lingers regardless of external circumstances, making relaxation feel nearly impossible. It may manifest as persistent worry, racing thoughts, or an underlying sense of tension that never fully dissipates. Chronic stress keeps the nervous system in a state of fight-or-flight, where the body is constantly on high alert. This can lead to physical symptoms such as headaches, muscle tension, digestive issues, or an increased heart rate, as well as emotional symptoms like irritability, difficulty concentrating, or feelings of being overwhelmed. When stress becomes a constant presence, it drains energy and clouds judgment, making it difficult to find joy or clarity in daily life. A spiritual detox helps release the accumulated tension, allowing for deep relaxation and a renewed sense of calm.

Another major sign that the soul is burdened with unresolved energy is emotional exhaustion. This is different from physical fatigue—it is a deep, soul-level tiredness that does not go away with rest or sleep. It feels like carrying an invisible weight, where even small tasks become overwhelming. Emotional exhaustion often results from suppressing feelings, avoiding difficult emotions, or absorbing negativity from others without a way to cleanse and release it. When emotional energy is drained, simple interactions can feel exhausting, and social engagement may become more of a burden than a source of connection. Many people experiencing spiritual burnout find themselves withdrawing from others, lacking motivation, or feeling a sense of numbness. It can also manifest as frequent mood swings, where one moment feels manageable, and the next is overwhelming. This occurs when unprocessed emotions linger beneath the surface, subtly affecting daily interactions and perceptions. A spiritual detox helps clear these lingering emotions, restoring balance and emotional resilience.

A clear sign of spiritual stagnation is a feeling of disconnection from one's purpose or sense of meaning. There may be a persistent sense of emptiness, as if something is missing, despite external achievements or progress. Activities that once brought joy may feel unfulfilling, and personal goals may begin to seem directionless. This often happens when internal clutter—negative beliefs, self-doubt, or unresolved trauma—blocks the connection to deeper desires and inner wisdom. For some, this disconnection appears as a lack of motivation, where even things they once cared deeply about no longer bring excitement. Others may feel lost, unsure of what truly makes them happy or what path to follow. When the spiritual body is weighed down, it becomes difficult to hear intuition or feel inspired. A spiritual detox clears away the mental and emotional fog, helping to reconnect with personal values, passions, and a greater sense of purpose.

The mind is a powerful tool, shaping how we experience the world. However, when negativity dominates thought patterns, it can create an ongoing cycle of self-sabotage and emotional distress. Recurring negative thoughts—such as self-criticism, fear, or doubt—are strong indicators that a spiritual detox is needed. Negative thought patterns can become deeply ingrained over time, often stemming from past experiences, societal conditioning, or unresolved emotional wounds. These thoughts may take the form of constant worry about the future, self-doubt that prevents personal growth, or an inner voice that constantly criticizes. Over time, these patterns become so familiar that they feel like truth, reinforcing a cycle of limitation and fear. A spiritual detox allows for the release of these ingrained thought patterns, creating space for new, empowering beliefs to take root. By cleansing the mind and energy field, it becomes easier to break free from the grip of self-doubt and step into a more confident, authentic version of oneself.

The sensation of being lost—disconnected from oneself, intuition, or a sense of something greater. This may manifest as an inability to trust personal instincts, a lack of clarity in decision-making, or an ongoing feeling of dissatisfaction that is difficult to define. For some, this feeling of disconnection appears as restlessness, a deep longing for something more without knowing what that "more" is. Others may experience a lack of emotional depth in their relationships, a sense of going through life on autopilot, or difficulty feeling present in the moment. When the spiritual body is out of alignment, the connection to personal truth, inner wisdom, and the flow of life becomes disrupted. A spiritual detox helps remove the layers of mental and emotional fog that contribute to this disconnection. It realigns energy, restores clarity, and strengthens the connection to intuition, allowing for a greater sense of trust in oneself and the path ahead.

A cluttered mind is another common sign that spiritual cleansing is needed. When mental energy is overloaded, it becomes difficult to concentrate, retain information, or make decisions with clarity. Overthinking, excessive worry, and an inability to quiet the mind are all indications that the mind is carrying too much mental clutter. This can result in difficulty staying present, as thoughts constantly jump from one concern to the next. People experiencing mental overload may find themselves struggling to focus on conversations, procrastinating on important tasks, or feeling paralyzed by indecision. A spiritual detox allows for a mental reset, creating space for clearer thinking, improved focus, and a renewed sense of peace.

If certain situations, people, or memories consistently provoke strong emotional reactions, it may indicate unresolved emotional blockages. When emotions remain unprocessed, they become stored within the body and mind, causing heightened sensitivity and unexpected triggers. For example, an offhand comment from someone may stir deep feelings of insecurity, or a specific situation may cause an overwhelming emotional response that seems disproportionate. These reactions often point to unresolved wounds that need attention and healing. A spiritual detox helps bring these suppressed emotions to the surface so they can be acknowledged, processed, and released, reducing emotional volatility and restoring inner balance.

Quality sleep is essential for both physical and spiritual well-being. When sleep patterns are disrupted—whether through insomnia, restless sleep, or frequent waking—it may be a sign that the subconscious is burdened with unresolved thoughts and emotions. Spiritual clutter can create an overactive mind, making it difficult to relax enough for deep, restorative sleep. It can also result in vivid dreams, nightmares, or waking up feeling just as exhausted as before sleeping. This indicates that the mind and spirit are not fully at rest, weighed down by lingering tension and unresolved energy. A spiritual detox helps calm the mind and restore balance, promoting deeper, more refreshing sleep.

Carrying an invisible weight that never fully lifts is one of the most subtle yet profound signs of needing a spiritual detox. This feeling can be difficult to describe but is often experienced as a sense of emotional burden, a lack of vibrancy, or a diminished sense of joy. This heaviness often results from absorbing too much negativity from external sources, whether through toxic relationships, media consumption, or stressful environments. Without regular cleansing, this energy accumulates, creating a sense of sluggishness, disconnection, and overall unease. A spiritual detox helps lighten this burden, creating space for renewed energy, joy, and emotional freedom.

These signs are invitations for healing rather than warnings of permanent imbalance. A spiritual detox provides the opportunity to clear what no longer serves, restoring a sense of peace, clarity, and connection. By acknowledging these signals, individuals can take proactive steps toward renewal, allowing for a more vibrant, balanced, and spiritually fulfilling life.

## How This Book Will Help

This book is designed as a comprehensive guide to spiritual detox, offering a structured yet flexible approach to clearing internal blockages, releasing negative energy, and realigning with a deeper sense of peace and purpose. It is not merely a theoretical discussion of spirituality but a practical roadmap that provides actionable steps for genuine transformation. By engaging with the tools and techniques within these pages, readers will find themselves equipped with the means to cleanse emotional, mental, and energetic clutter, fostering clarity and inner balance.

The process of spiritual detoxification requires both awareness and action. Throughout this book, readers will be guided through a variety of methods to release stagnant energy and cultivate a renewed sense of connection with themselves and the world around them. Practical steps will be outlined in a clear and approachable manner, ensuring that anyone, regardless of their spiritual background or experience, can integrate these techniques into their daily life. These steps are designed to help individuals recognize the weight they may be carrying—whether from past experiences, limiting beliefs, or external influences—and provide them with effective strategies for letting go.

One of the most powerful tools for spiritual cleansing is meditation. This book will introduce a series of guided meditations specifically crafted to assist in the detoxification process. These meditations are structured to help quiet the mind, release emotional blockages, and create space for deeper self-awareness. Whether the reader is new to meditation or has an established practice, these guided exercises will serve as a foundation for healing, allowing them to reconnect with their inner self and cultivate a sense of calm amidst life's challenges.

Reflection is another key component of the detox journey. Throughout the book, readers will find a variety of reflective exercises designed to encourage deep introspection. These exercises will prompt readers to examine their thoughts, emotions, and beliefs, uncovering patterns that may be holding them back. By engaging in this process of self-inquiry, individuals will gain clarity on what aspects of their lives require healing and transformation. These reflections will not only highlight areas in need of detox but also provide a path toward lasting change.

Healing techniques woven throughout this book will address multiple levels of spiritual detox, offering a holistic approach to renewal. Some techniques will focus on energetic cleansing—helping readers clear stagnant or negative energy that may be lingering in their spiritual field. Others will emphasize emotional release, providing safe and effective ways to process unresolved emotions and let go of past wounds. Additionally, mental detox strategies will be included, offering guidance on how to shift limiting beliefs, quiet an overactive mind, and create a healthier inner dialogue. These techniques are intended to be practical and adaptable, allowing readers to tailor their approach based on their individual needs and preferences.

Spiritual detox is a deeply personal journey, and the methods presented here are designed to be accessible and adaptable. Readers can move through the book at their own pace, selecting the practices that feel most relevant to their current state of being. Whether they prefer a structured routine or a more intuitive approach, this book provides the flexibility to engage with spiritual detox in a way that feels authentic and effective.

Ultimately, this book serves as both a guide and a companion on the journey to spiritual renewal. It will support readers in shedding what no longer serves them, creating space for clarity, peace, and deeper connection. By following the practices outlined within these pages, individuals will discover not only how to detox their spiritual energy but also how to maintain a state of inner balance and harmony. The goal is not just temporary relief but a lasting transformation—one that fosters greater well-being, emotional freedom, and a deeper alignment with one's true self.

# Understanding Your Spiritual Energy

*"Your energy is the language of your soul—learn to listen, and it will guide you toward balance and healing."*

**Understanding Your Spiritual Energy**

Spiritual energy is the unseen force that flows through every living being, shaping thoughts, emotions, and experiences in ways both subtle and profound. It is the essence that animates life, often described as a vibration, a frequency, or a current of energy that connects individuals to the universe, to one another, and to their higher selves. While intangible, its presence is undeniable, influencing mood, intuition, and even physical health. Some traditions refer to it as life force, prana, chi, or soul energy, but regardless of the name, the fundamental concept remains the same: it is the vital essence that sustains and influences all aspects of existence.

At its core, spiritual energy is dynamic, constantly shifting in response to thoughts, emotions, and external circumstances. Just as physical energy can be depleted through exhaustion and stress, spiritual energy is equally susceptible to drain, imbalance, or stagnation. When it flows freely, there is a sense of clarity, purpose, and harmony with life. When blocked or disrupted, feelings of heaviness, confusion, and emotional distress can emerge. This energy does not exist in isolation; rather, it intertwines with the mental, emotional, and physical aspects of being, forming an interconnected system where balance is key.

Vibrations are often used to describe the quality of spiritual energy, as everything in the universe operates at a frequency. High vibrations are associated with love, joy, peace, and gratitude, while lower vibrations correspond to fear, anger, resentment, and despair. The state of one's energy directly influences interactions with the world—those who maintain high vibrations often experience more positivity, synchronicities, and an innate sense of well-being, while those stuck in lower vibrations may struggle with negativity, disconnection, and an overwhelming sense of heaviness. Understanding these frequencies is the first step toward harnessing spiritual energy in a way that nurtures personal growth and healing.

Because spiritual energy is affected by internal and external influences, maintaining its balance requires awareness and conscious effort. Negative thoughts, unresolved trauma, toxic environments, and even certain foods or substances can weigh down energy, creating an internal fog that dulls intuition and emotional clarity. On the other hand, practices such as meditation, breathwork, mindfulness, and connection with nature can elevate and restore energy, creating an environment where the spirit can thrive. Recognizing these shifts and understanding their impact is essential for cultivating a state of energetic well-being.

The relationship between spiritual energy and overall well-being is profound. When energy is aligned and flowing harmoniously, there is an innate sense of peace, resilience, and vitality. It becomes easier to navigate challenges, process emotions, and connect with one's purpose. However, when energy is fragmented, scattered, or blocked, it can manifest as persistent fatigue, anxiety, or a feeling of being stuck in life. By deepening awareness of this energy and learning how to work with it rather than against it, individuals can begin to clear away internal blockages and create space for healing and renewal.

Every person has the ability to sense and influence their own energy, though many go through life unaware of this power. By tuning into the subtle shifts in vibration, paying attention to how certain environments, thoughts, or people affect their state of being, and actively engaging in practices that nurture spiritual vitality, it becomes possible to reclaim control over one's inner world. Awareness is the key to transformation, and with it comes the ability to cultivate a life filled with greater clarity, peace, and alignment with one's highest self.

## How Energy Becomes Blocked

Spiritual energy, though powerful and ever-present, is not immune to disruptions. It can become stagnant, blocked, or depleted due to various internal and external factors, leading to emotional, mental, and even physical distress. When energy is obstructed, the natural flow that connects individuals to their higher selves, to others, and to the universe is weakened, creating an inner resistance that makes clarity, peace, and spiritual alignment difficult to attain. Understanding how energy blockages occur is the first step toward clearing them and restoring balance.

One of the most common causes of blocked energy is unresolved trauma. Painful experiences, whether from childhood or adulthood, can leave deep imprints on the energetic body, causing a lingering sense of fear, sadness, or distrust. Trauma has a way of embedding itself in the subconscious, forming energetic knots that restrict the free flow of spiritual vitality. These blockages can manifest as feelings of emotional numbness, unexplained anxiety, or a persistent inability to move forward in life. Often, these wounds remain buried beneath the surface, influencing behavior, relationships, and self-perception in ways that may not be immediately recognized.

Limiting beliefs also contribute to energy stagnation. These deeply ingrained thoughts—often inherited from family, society, or past experiences—shape how individuals perceive themselves and their potential. Messages such as "I am not good enough," "I don't deserve happiness," or "Life is always a struggle" act as energetic barriers that prevent expansion and growth. Each limiting belief reinforces patterns of self-doubt and fear, restricting the ability to embrace new opportunities, trust intuition, or step into personal power. Over time, these beliefs can form a rigid energetic structure that confines individuals within a cycle of repetitive struggles.

Emotional wounds, especially those left unprocessed, create another layer of energy blockages. Feelings of grief, anger, betrayal, or shame, when suppressed or ignored, do not simply fade away; they embed themselves within the energetic field, subtly influencing thoughts and emotions. Holding onto unresolved pain can weigh down the spirit, making joy and lightness feel out of reach. It may also lead to repeated emotional patterns, where the same types of struggles, conflicts, or disappointments continue to arise, seemingly without explanation. These cycles are often the result of trapped emotional energy seeking expression and resolution.

External negativity further compounds energy blockages. Just as the body absorbs nutrients from food, the energetic body absorbs frequencies from its surroundings. Toxic environments, unhealthy relationships, or constant exposure to negativity—whether through the media, social interactions, or personal experiences—can gradually erode spiritual well-being. Being in the presence of those who drain energy, manipulate emotions, or project their own pain onto others can lead to a gradual dimming of one's own vitality. Over time, this exposure can create a dense energetic field, making it difficult to remain centered, optimistic, or connected to higher awareness.

Recognizing energy blockages requires tuning into the body, mind, and emotions with honesty and self-awareness. Feelings of fatigue, restlessness, chronic stress, or a sense of being stuck often indicate energetic disruptions. Persistent negative thoughts, difficulty concentrating, or an inability to feel excitement for life may also signal an imbalance. By identifying these blockages, it becomes possible to begin the process of release, creating space for energy to flow freely once more. Clearing these obstructions is an essential step toward spiritual detoxification, allowing for renewal, healing, and a deeper connection to one's true essence.

**Chakras and Energy Flow**

The human body is more than just a physical form; it is an intricate network of energy, vibrations, and frequencies that influence every aspect of life. Ancient traditions and modern spiritual practices recognize the presence of an energy system that extends beyond the physical realm. This system is often described through the framework of chakras—seven energy centers that run along the spine, each governing different aspects of physical, emotional, and spiritual well-being. These chakras act as conduits for life force energy, also known as prana, chi, or universal energy, allowing vitality to flow through the body.

When energy moves freely, it fosters balance, clarity, and a deep sense of peace. However, daily stress, emotional wounds, and external negativity can create blockages, disrupting the natural flow of energy. These blockages can manifest in many ways—fatigue, anxiety, lack of motivation, difficulty in relationships, or even physical ailments. Understanding the chakras and their role in spiritual health is the first step toward achieving balance and harmony within oneself.

## The Root Chakra (Muladhara)

Located at the base of the spine, the root chakra is the foundation of the energy system. It governs stability, security, and survival instincts. When the root chakra is balanced, there is a strong sense of groundedness and trust in life's journey. A well-functioning root chakra helps individuals feel safe, secure, and capable of handling life's challenges.

When imbalanced, however, the root chakra can create feelings of anxiety, restlessness, or financial insecurity. On a physical level, blockages may manifest as lower back pain, immune system issues, or problems with the legs and feet. People with a blocked root chakra may struggle with a deep-seated fear of instability, often feeling disconnected from their physical body or overwhelmed by stress.

Healing the root chakra involves grounding exercises such as walking barefoot on natural surfaces, practicing mindfulness, and using affirmations like "I am safe. I am supported. I am grounded." Eating root vegetables, wearing red, and engaging in physical movement can also help restore balance.

## The Sacral Chakra (Svadhisthana)

Just below the navel lies the sacral chakra, which is associated with creativity, passion, pleasure, and emotional expression. This chakra governs relationships, sensuality, and the ability to embrace change. A balanced sacral chakra allows one to experience joy, pursue creative endeavors, and connect deeply with others.

When blocked, individuals may experience emotional suppression, guilt, fear of intimacy, or a creative block. On a physical level, imbalances can manifest as reproductive health issues, lower back pain, or digestive problems.

Restoring balance to the sacral chakra involves engaging in creative activities, dancing, expressing emotions freely, and practicing self-care. Water-related activities, such as swimming or bathing, can also support sacral chakra healing.

## The Solar Plexus Chakra (Manipura)

Located in the upper abdomen, the solar plexus chakra is the center of personal power, confidence, and self-discipline. It governs motivation, decision-making, and the ability to take action. A balanced solar plexus chakra instills a sense of purpose and determination, helping individuals feel in control of their lives.

When this chakra is blocked, self-doubt, procrastination, and low self-esteem can arise. People may struggle with setting boundaries, asserting themselves, or overcoming fears. On a physical level, imbalances may manifest as digestive issues, chronic fatigue, or metabolic disorders.

Healing this chakra involves practices that boost confidence, such as setting personal goals, engaging in affirmations like "I am strong. I am capable. I am worthy.", and engaging in core-strengthening exercises. The color yellow, sunlight exposure, and deep breathing exercises also help balance the solar plexus.

**The Heart Chakra (Anahata)**

The heart chakra, positioned at the center of the chest, serves as the bridge between the physical and spiritual realms. It is the source of love, compassion, and emotional connection. A balanced heart chakra allows for deep, meaningful relationships, self-love, and empathy.

When blocked, individuals may struggle with resentment, heartbreak, loneliness, or fear of vulnerability. Holding onto past pain or suppressing emotions can create energetic stagnation in this area. Physically, an imbalanced heart chakra may contribute to heart problems, respiratory issues, or poor circulation.

To heal the heart chakra, engaging in loving-kindness meditation, practicing forgiveness, and expressing gratitude can help. Surrounding oneself with green nature, engaging in acts of kindness, and using affirmations like "I give and receive love freely." can also be powerful tools for restoration.

**The Throat Chakra (Vishuddha)**

The throat chakra governs communication, self-expression, and authenticity. It enables individuals to speak their truth and connect with others through honest dialogue. A balanced throat chakra allows for clear, confident, and thoughtful communication.

When blocked, people may feel unheard, struggle to express themselves, or fear speaking up. They may also experience social anxiety, dishonesty, or excessive shyness. Physical symptoms of imbalance include throat pain, frequent colds, or thyroid issues.

Healing the throat chakra involves speaking positive affirmations, singing, journaling, and practicing mindful listening. The color blue, drinking herbal teas, and breathwork can also support throat chakra balance.

## The Third Eye Chakra (Ajna)

Located between the eyebrows, the third eye chakra is the center of intuition, insight, and spiritual wisdom. It governs perception, imagination, and the ability to see beyond the physical world. A balanced third eye chakra enhances clarity, decision-making, and inner knowing.

When blocked, people may experience confusion, lack of direction, difficulty trusting their intuition, or an overactive mind filled with self-doubt. Physical symptoms can include headaches, eye strain, or sleep disturbances.

To balance the third eye chakra, meditation, visualization, and dream journaling can be beneficial. Practicing mindfulness, limiting screen time, and focusing on deep self-reflection can also enhance intuitive clarity.

## The Crown Chakra (Sahasrara)

At the top of the head, the crown chakra represents higher consciousness, divine wisdom, and spiritual enlightenment. It is the gateway to cosmic awareness and a deep sense of universal connection. A balanced crown chakra fosters inner peace, heightened awareness, and spiritual fulfillment.

Blockages in the crown chakra may cause feelings of disconnection, lack of purpose, or existential doubt. Physically, it may manifest as chronic migraines, sensitivity to light, or neurological imbalances.

Healing this chakra involves meditation, prayer, and time spent in silence. Using the color violet or white, engaging in gratitude practices, and surrendering to the flow of life can help align the crown chakra with higher consciousness.

The chakras are deeply interconnected, and an imbalance in one can create disruptions in others. By understanding how these energy centers function and influence daily life, individuals can cultivate a balanced energy system that supports spiritual clarity, emotional well-being, and a deepened connection with the universe. Practices like meditation, breathwork, and energy healing can help remove blockages and restore the natural flow of energy, leading to profound transformation on all levels—body, mind, and spirit.

**Guided Meditation**

To begin with, find a quiet and comfortable space where you won't be disturbed. You may sit cross-legged on the floor, lie down on your back, or settle into a comfortable chair with your feet firmly planted on the ground. Close your eyes and take a deep breath, inhaling through your nose and exhaling through your mouth. As you breathe, allow your body to relax, releasing any tension in your shoulders, neck, or jaw. With each exhale, feel yourself letting go of the stresses of the day, becoming fully present in this moment.

Begin by bringing your awareness to your breath. Notice the natural rhythm of your inhalations and exhalations without trying to control them. Imagine your breath as a wave, gently rising and falling, moving through your body with ease. As you continue to breathe deeply, visualize a warm, radiant light surrounding your entire being. This light serves as a protective and healing force, allowing you to safely explore your energy field.

Now, direct your attention to the top of your head, the crown chakra. This is the energy center associated with spiritual connection, wisdom, and higher consciousness. Imagine a brilliant violet or white light gently flowing into the top of your head, filling your mind with clarity and peace. Notice any sensations—does this area feel open and expansive, or do you sense heaviness, pressure, or discomfort? If you feel any resistance, simply acknowledge it without judgment. Breathe deeply into this space, allowing the light to clear any energetic blockages.

Slowly move your awareness downward to your third eye, located between your eyebrows. This energy center governs intuition, perception, and inner knowing. Tune in to any sensations—do you feel a sense of clarity and insight, or does this area feel clouded and tense? If you notice a blockage, visualize a soft indigo light dissolving any fogginess, allowing your inner vision to become clear and strong.

Next, shift your focus to your throat chakra, the center of communication and self-expression. Many people hold unspoken words, fears, or suppressed emotions in this area, creating energetic constriction. Observe whether your throat feels tight, dry, or tense. If you sense a blockage, imagine a bright blue light expanding within your throat, gently releasing any stored emotions or unexpressed truths. As you breathe, visualize your throat opening like a blossoming flower, allowing clear, honest, and confident expression.

Now, bring your attention to your heart chakra, the energetic center of love, compassion, and emotional healing. This is where grief, heartbreak, or unresolved emotions may reside. Tune into this space—does your heart feel open and full, or do you sense a tightness or heaviness? If there is emotional tension, imagine a soft green or pink light gently radiating through your chest, dissolving pain and inviting in love, forgiveness, and warmth. With each inhale, allow your heart to expand, and with each exhale, release anything that no longer serves you.

Continue your journey downward to your solar plexus, the core of your personal power and self-confidence. This chakra governs your sense of self, willpower, and motivation. If you feel a knot in your stomach, unease, or a sense of being stuck, it may indicate an energetic blockage in this area. Visualize a golden light igniting in your solar plexus, like the radiant sun, burning away fear, doubt, or insecurity. Allow this energy to strengthen your confidence and sense of direction.

Moving lower, shift your focus to your sacral chakra, located just below your navel. This is the center of creativity, passion, and emotional flow. If you've been feeling uninspired, emotionally overwhelmed, or disconnected from your desires, there may be an energy blockage here. Imagine a warm, orange light flowing like water, washing away stagnation and allowing creativity and joy to return. With each breath, let this energy expand, reigniting passion and emotional balance.

Finally, bring your attention to your root chakra, located at the base of your spine. This is your foundation, the center of stability, security, and grounding. Feel into this space—does it feel strong and rooted, or do you sense fear, instability, or unease? If this area feels blocked, visualize a deep red energy anchoring you to the earth, providing you with strength, safety, and stability. Imagine roots extending from your body into the ground, connecting you to the earth's nourishing energy.

As you complete this scan, take a few more deep breaths, allowing any identified blockages to release with each exhale. Imagine your entire body glowing with balanced, harmonious energy. Feel a sense of lightness, clarity, and peace. When you feel ready, gently bring your awareness back to the present moment. Wiggle your fingers and toes, stretch your body slightly, and slowly open your eyes. Carry this newfound awareness with you, knowing that you can return to this practice whenever you need to realign your energy and reconnect with yourself.

**Journaling Exercise**

Journaling is a powerful tool for self-discovery, allowing you to explore your inner world and uncover hidden patterns that may be affecting your energy. Writing about your experiences creates space for clarity, healing, and transformation. This exercise will help you reflect on moments when you have felt drained, disconnected, or energetically depleted. By examining these experiences, you can identify the root causes of your energy imbalances, whether they stem from emotional wounds, external influences, or personal habits.

Before you begin writing, find a quiet, comfortable space where you won't be disturbed. Grab a journal or a blank piece of paper and a pen. You may also choose to use a digital journaling app if that feels more natural. Take a few deep breaths to center yourself, allowing your mind to settle into a state of introspection. If you find it helpful, set the mood with soft instrumental music, light a candle, or diffuse calming essential oils like lavender or frankincense. Creating an intentional space for self-reflection can enhance the depth of your writing.

Begin by recalling specific moments when you felt energetically drained, emotionally numb, or disconnected from yourself and others. Think about times when you struggled to find motivation, felt overwhelmed, or sensed a lack of joy. These moments may be fleeting or prolonged periods of exhaustion. Consider whether you have ever walked into a space and immediately felt exhausted or uncomfortable, or if you have left a conversation feeling mentally and emotionally depleted. Reflect on whether certain relationships consistently leave you feeling drained rather than uplifted. Notice if you experience cycles of burnout, where your energy crashes after periods of stress, or if you have felt disconnected from your passions, creativity, or sense of purpose. Write about these experiences in as much detail as possible. Describe what was happening, where you were, who was involved, and how you felt emotionally, mentally, and physically. The goal is to bring awareness to patterns that may have previously gone unnoticed.

Once you have written about these moments, begin to explore what might have caused them. Energy imbalances can stem from many sources, including emotional wounds, negative thought patterns, external negativity, or even subconscious beliefs that limit your growth. Reflect on whether you were in an environment filled with negativity, tension, or stress, or if you were taking on the emotions or burdens of others without realizing it.

Consider if unresolved emotions, such as guilt, resentment, or fear, contributed to your exhaustion. Think about whether you were ignoring your own needs in order to meet the expectations of others, or if you have been in relationships where you gave more than you received, leaving you depleted. Ask yourself if you have habits that drain your energy, such as excessive social media use, overworking, or lack of sleep. Write openly and honestly about any insights that arise. If certain themes keep recurring, take note of them—they may indicate deeper energy blockages that require healing.

The body often provides signals when something is energetically off balance. Paying attention to these signs can help you become more aware of when your energy is being affected. Notice if you feel tension in your body, such as tight shoulders, a heavy chest, or a pit in your stomach. Reflect on whether you have experienced chronic fatigue, headaches, or unexplained physical discomfort. Observe if your mood shifts dramatically, leading to feelings of irritability, sadness, or anxiety. Consider whether you feel mentally foggy, unfocused, or uninspired. If any of these signs resonate, take a moment to reflect on how they relate to your energy state. Write about how your body has reacted to stressful or emotionally charged situations in the past. Developing awareness of these patterns will help you recognize energy drains earlier in the future.

Now that you've identified moments of energy depletion and their potential causes, it's time to focus on what restores your energy. Think about times when you have felt uplifted, recharged, and aligned with your highest self. Reflect on what activities make you feel alive and inspired, whether there are people in your life who energize and support you, and when you feel the most at peace and connected to yourself. Consider whether you have engaged in practices like meditation, deep breathing, or time in nature that made you feel renewed. Think about what small shifts you could make in your daily life to protect and restore your energy. Write about these moments and what made them so energizing. This will help you build a toolbox of strategies for maintaining a balanced and vibrant energy field.

To complete the exercise, write down an intention or affirmation that will help you protect your energy moving forward. Your intention can be a simple, empowering statement such as "I honor my energy and release what no longer serves me," "I set healthy boundaries that protect my peace and well-being," or "I am mindful of where I direct my energy and choose only what uplifts me." Writing your intention solidifies your commitment to self-care and spiritual well-being. Keep it somewhere visible—on a sticky note, in your phone, or as a daily reminder in your journal.

This journaling practice is more than just an exercise; it is a tool for deepening your awareness and healing your energy. As you revisit it over time, you will gain new insights and become more attuned to the shifts in your energetic state. By acknowledging what drains and restores you, you empower yourself to make conscious choices that support your spiritual and emotional well-being.

# Releasing Negative Attachments

*"You cannot heal in the same place where your pain was born—set yourself free by releasing what no longer serves you."*

**Identifying Negative Attachments**

Negative attachments can take many forms, often embedding themselves so deeply into our daily lives that we fail to recognize their presence. They drain our energy, cloud our judgment, and prevent us from living with clarity and peace. These attachments can stem from toxic relationships, unresolved traumas, limiting thought patterns, or even societal conditioning that dictates how we should think, act, and feel. Identifying these negative influences is the first step toward releasing them and reclaiming your spiritual energy.

Toxic relationships are among the most common sources of negative attachments. These can exist in any area of life—romantic partnerships, friendships, family dynamics, or even professional environments. A toxic relationship is not always overtly abusive; it can be subtly draining, leaving you feeling emotionally exhausted, unappreciated, or manipulated. Sometimes, people stay in these relationships out of obligation, fear, or familiarity, even when they know the connection is unhealthy. Reflecting on how you feel after interacting with someone can reveal whether they are a source of nourishment or depletion. If you constantly feel anxious, guilty, or unworthy after engaging with a particular person, it may be a sign that the relationship is negatively affecting your spiritual well-being.

Past traumas also create deeply rooted attachments that affect emotional and spiritual health. Unresolved pain from childhood experiences, past relationships, or significant life events can linger in the subconscious, influencing behaviors and thought patterns. Trauma often manifests as fear, self-doubt, or difficulty trusting others. Some individuals unconsciously recreate past wounds in new situations, feeling drawn to relationships or environments that mirror their unresolved pain. This cycle can be difficult to recognize, but acknowledging past wounds is essential to breaking free from their grip. Healing does not mean forgetting or invalidating experiences; rather, it involves processing emotions, accepting what has happened, and choosing to move forward without allowing the past to dictate the present.

Unhealthy thought patterns can be just as binding as toxic relationships or past traumas. Negative self-talk, self-sabotage, and limiting beliefs shape our reality by reinforcing ideas that restrict personal growth. Thoughts such as "I am not good enough," "I will never be happy," or "I always fail" become self-fulfilling prophecies, trapping individuals in cycles of doubt and fear. These mental patterns often develop from external influences—family expectations, societal norms, or past failures—but over time, they become ingrained as personal truths. The mind is incredibly powerful, and what we repeatedly tell ourselves shapes our experience of life. Recognizing these destructive narratives and replacing them with empowering affirmations is a vital step in detaching from mental constraints.

Societal conditioning plays a significant role in shaping beliefs and attachments. From an early age, individuals are taught what is acceptable, desirable, or expected. Cultural norms dictate how people should behave, what success looks like, and what is considered valuable. While some societal structures provide guidance and stability, others impose limitations that suppress individuality and inner peace. Many people find themselves chasing goals they do not truly desire, conforming to roles that do not align with their spirit, or suppressing emotions to meet social expectations. This creates an internal conflict that leads to spiritual exhaustion. Recognizing when external pressures dictate personal choices allows for greater autonomy in shaping a life that aligns with one's authentic self.

By identifying negative attachments, you take the first step toward freeing yourself from their influence. Awareness alone does not break these chains, but it creates the space for transformation. Once you recognize what is holding you back, you can begin the process of releasing, healing, and reclaiming your energy.

**The Emotional Weight of the Past:**

The past carries an immense emotional weight, often lingering in ways that quietly shape our present experiences. Unresolved emotions such as resentment, guilt, and regret can act as invisible chains, restricting spiritual growth and preventing true inner peace. Holding onto these emotions keeps the past alive in our minds, influencing our decisions, interactions, and self-perception. While painful experiences are an inevitable part of life, the way we process and carry them determines whether they serve as stepping stones for growth or barriers to our evolution.

Resentment is one of the heaviest emotional burdens a person can carry. It arises from perceived injustices, betrayals, or unresolved conflicts, creating an ongoing loop of anger and frustration. When left unaddressed, resentment festers, taking root in the subconscious and affecting how we view the world. It can distort perceptions, making it difficult to trust others or approach life with openness. Resentment does not punish those who have wronged us—it only poisons the one holding onto it. The energy required to maintain anger toward someone drains spiritual reserves, leaving little room for joy, clarity, or connection. Releasing resentment does not mean condoning the actions of others; rather, it is a conscious choice to free oneself from the suffering attached to the past.

Guilt, on the other hand, arises when we believe we have caused harm, failed to meet expectations, or acted against our values. While guilt can sometimes serve as a moral compass, guiding us toward self-reflection and growth, excessive guilt becomes paralyzing. It creates a sense of unworthiness and self-punishment, preventing individuals from fully embracing their potential. Some people hold onto guilt for years, replaying mistakes in their minds and believing they do not deserve forgiveness. However, true spiritual healing requires self-compassion. Every human being makes mistakes, and growth is only possible when we allow ourselves the grace to learn and evolve. Holding onto guilt does not change the past—it only robs the present of peace.

Regret is another emotional weight that often lingers, tied to missed opportunities, lost relationships, or choices that did not lead to the desired outcome. Regret keeps people trapped in the "what if" mindset, constantly wondering how life might have been different had they made other decisions. This cycle of thinking fuels dissatisfaction, preventing appreciation for the present moment. The truth is, every choice made in the past was based on the knowledge, emotions, and circumstances available at that time. Instead of dwelling on what could have been, spiritual growth involves accepting past decisions and recognizing that they were necessary for personal evolution. The past cannot be rewritten, but the lessons it offers can shape a more intentional and fulfilling future.

Carrying resentment, guilt, or regret places a heavy burden on the soul, creating energetic blockages that hinder spiritual progress. These emotions become part of an inner dialogue, reinforcing limiting beliefs and negative self-perceptions. However, healing begins when we acknowledge the weight we are carrying and make the choice to release it. Letting go does not mean erasing the past or denying emotions—it means allowing them to be processed, understood, and then set free. Through self-forgiveness, acceptance, and a commitment to living in the present, it is possible to lighten the emotional load and create space for greater clarity, peace, and spiritual expansion.

**Cord Cutting Ritual**

Energy ties form between people, experiences, and thoughts, often without conscious awareness. These energetic cords represent emotional and spiritual connections that can either nourish or drain us. Some bonds bring love, support, and strength, while others carry lingering pain, resentment, or attachment that prevents true healing. There are connections we cherish, ones that uplift and inspire us, but there are also those that hold us back, keeping us trapped in old cycles of suffering. When we remain tied to past relationships, painful memories, or even limiting beliefs, we carry an invisible weight that restricts our growth and prevents us from fully stepping into our potential. Releasing these ties is not about erasing the past or denying what was, but rather about allowing ourselves the freedom to move forward without being weighed down by energies that no longer serve our highest good.

Before performing a cord-cutting ritual, it is important to enter the right mindset. Energy work requires presence, clarity, and deep intention. The effectiveness of any spiritual practice lies in the level of focus and sincerity brought to it. This ritual is not performed out of anger or a desire for vengeance; it is done with love, respect, and a genuine commitment to healing. A quiet, undisturbed space is essential, one where the mind can settle and the heart can open to the process of release. The energies we seek to sever are often deeply ingrained, tied to emotions that have shaped us for years or even decades. Letting them go requires a level of readiness, an acknowledgment that we deserve peace more than we need to hold onto the past.

Bringing a few symbolic items into the ritual can deepen its impact. A white candle represents purity, clarity, and new beginnings, helping to illuminate the path ahead. A black candle can serve as a symbol of transformation, absorbing negative energy and dissolving what no longer aligns with our true self. Crystals such as black tourmaline or obsidian can assist in clearing away energetic debris, while selenite offers a purifying effect, ensuring that what is released does not linger in our energetic field. Water, a powerful conduit of spiritual cleansing, can be used to wash away residual ties, either through a ritual bath or simply by washing one's hands in a bowl of water after the practice is complete. Some choose to incorporate a piece of string or ribbon, a physical representation of the cord that is about to be severed, which can be cut as a tangible act of release.

Settling into a comfortable position, taking deep, measured breaths, and turning inward is the first step. Closing the eyes, feeling the rise and fall of each inhale and exhale, the body gradually relaxes as awareness shifts away from the outside world and into the deeper layers of the self. Bringing to mind the person, memory, or belief that is to be released, a moment is taken to fully acknowledge its presence. There is no need to rush this part of the process. Some attachments have been carried for so long that they have become part of one's identity, and letting them go can feel like losing a piece of oneself. Honoring the emotions that arise, allowing them to be felt without resistance, is essential. The heart knows when it is ready, and it will communicate that readiness in its own time.

Once the connection is clearly visualized, an energy cord can be imagined stretching between the self and the other entity. It may appear as a glowing thread of light, a thick rope, a chain, or even a delicate vine. Each person's experience is unique, and there is no right or wrong way to perceive this energy. Observing its texture, its weight, and where it is attached in the body offers insight into the nature of the bond. Some cords may be wrapped tightly around the heart, representing a deep emotional tie, while others may be linked to the throat, indicating an unspoken truth or suppressed words. Certain cords may stem from the mind, showing how thoughts and beliefs have kept the connection alive.

Surrounding oneself in golden-white light, feeling its warmth spreading from the crown of the head to the tips of the toes, creates a protective field. This light acts as a shield, strengthening the spirit and clearing away residual negativity. If a higher power, spiritual guides, ancestors, or angels are part of one's belief system, they can be called upon to witness and support the release. There is great power in knowing that one is not alone in this process.

When the moment feels right, the cord is severed. Some may envision themselves holding a sword made of light, a silver blade, or a fiery arrow, each representing a personal tool of energetic release. With a decisive motion, the cord is cut. If a physical ribbon or string is being used, this is the moment to take scissors and make a clean break. As the cord dissolves, it is not destroyed in anger, but instead returned to the universe, transformed into neutral energy. There is no need to wish harm upon the person or situation that was released. The goal is not revenge or avoidance, but liberation.

After the cord has been cut, the space where it once existed must be filled with healing energy. Taking both hands and placing them over the heart, breathing deeply, and visualizing a soft, radiant light flowing into the space left behind ensures that nothing negative lingers. Whispering a final affirmation to oneself, reinforcing the freedom that has just been claimed, is an important final step. Words such as "I release this with love," "I reclaim my energy," or "I am whole, I am free" carry immense power in solidifying the transformation that has taken place.

To close the ritual, a grounding practice is necessary. Walking barefoot on the earth, drinking a glass of water, or holding a grounding stone such as hematite or red jasper can help the body integrate the energetic shift. The body may feel lighter, as though a weight has been lifted, or there may be a sense of quiet emptiness where the connection once was. This is normal. Over the following days, paying attention to emotional changes, shifts in thought patterns, or a newfound sense of peace is essential. If old feelings resurface, it is not a sign that the ritual did not work—it is simply the mind and body adjusting to the absence of the energy that was once present.

Cord-cutting is a practice of deep self-respect. It is an acknowledgment that holding on to certain energies does not serve growth, peace, or happiness. The past will always be a part of one's journey, but it does not have to define the future. Some ties are meant to be honored and released so that new opportunities, relationships, and experiences can take their place. There is a profound beauty in knowing that by letting go, space is created for something even greater to enter.

**Guided Meditation**

Letting go of emotional baggage requires more than just a desire to move forward; it demands a conscious and intentional release of the energies that have been weighing you down. By immersing yourself in visualization, you will create a powerful shift within your energy field, clearing space for new, positive experiences.

Find a quiet space where you won't be disturbed. This is your time—your moment to release the weight you have been carrying. Sit or lie down in a comfortable position, allowing your body to fully relax. Close your eyes gently, and take a slow, deep breath in through your nose. Feel the air expand in your lungs, filling every space within you. Hold for a few seconds, then exhale slowly through your mouth. With that exhale, imagine releasing any tension, stress, or heaviness you have been holding.

Continue breathing deeply, allowing your inhales to draw in fresh energy, and your exhales to push out anything stagnant within you. With each breath, your body softens, your mind quiets, and your spirit begins to open.

Now, visualize yourself standing in a tranquil, sacred space. This place is yours alone—perhaps a lush green meadow bathed in golden sunlight, a quiet mountain peak where the wind gently hums, or a still lake reflecting the sky's endless depth. Wherever you are, feel the natural elements surrounding you. Notice the scent of the air, the temperature against your skin, and the gentle sounds that create an atmosphere of complete serenity.

As you stand in this sacred place, become aware of your energy field. Imagine a soft glow surrounding your body, like an aura of pure light. This light represents your essence—your thoughts, emotions, and spirit. Take a moment to feel into this energy. Does it feel heavy or light? Is it smooth and flowing, or does it feel tangled and weighed down? Without judgment, simply observe.

Now, picture thin, delicate cords extending outward from your body. These cords connect you to various people, experiences, emotions, and thoughts. Some may feel light and uplifting, while others may feel thick, dark, or restrictive. These are the attachments that no longer serve you—the emotional burdens, toxic relationships, lingering fears, or self-limiting beliefs that keep you tied to the past.

Gently trace your awareness along these cords, identifying the ones that feel the heaviest. Do you sense a relationship that drains your energy? A painful memory that still lingers? A fear that whispers doubts in your mind? Let these realizations surface naturally, without force.

Now, visualize a golden light beginning to radiate from within your heart. This light is warm, powerful, and filled with healing energy. It pulses outward, illuminating each of the cords connected to you. The ones that no longer serve your highest good begin to stand out—they are ready to be released.

In your hands, imagine a sacred tool given to you by the universe—perhaps a shimmering sword of light, a glowing crystal, or even the energy of your own hands, empowered with divine strength. Feel its weight, its warmth, its purpose. This tool is here to assist you in freeing yourself.

When you feel ready, begin to cut the cords one by one. With each cut, speak gently in your mind: "I release you with love. I reclaim my energy. I am free." As the cord dissolves, watch as it transforms into soft, golden dust, carried away by the breeze.

Take your time. There is no rush. With every release, notice how your body feels—perhaps lighter, more open, or even emotional as years of stored energy begin to clear. If any resistance arises, remind yourself that letting go does not mean forgetting or dismissing the past—it simply means choosing freedom over attachment.

Once all the necessary cords have been released, visualize your energy field glowing brighter than before. Any spaces left behind are now filling with healing light, sealing and restoring you. You are whole. You are free.

Take a deep breath in, allowing this new lightness to settle into your being. Exhale any last remnants of the past. Stay here for a moment, basking in the peace of your renewed energy.

When you feel ready, begin to bring awareness back to your physical body. Wiggle your fingers and toes, gently stretch your arms. As you open your eyes, take a moment to feel the difference within you. Carry this feeling with you, knowing that you have released what no longer serves you and made space for new beginnings.

**Journaling Exercise**

Find a quiet space where you feel safe, where distractions won't interrupt this deeply personal exercise. You may want to set the mood by dimming the lights, lighting a candle, or playing soft instrumental music. Before you begin writing, take a few deep breaths. With each inhale, invite clarity into your mind; with each exhale, release tension. Allow yourself to settle into the moment, feeling fully present with your emotions.

Open your journal, and give yourself permission to be completely honest. This is a sacred space—one where you don't have to filter your thoughts or worry about how they might be received. You are writing not to send these letters, but to confront, express, and ultimately let go of the emotions that have remained unspoken.

Begin by thinking about what or who you need to release. It may be a past version of yourself—perhaps one who was lost, struggling, or burdened by pain. Maybe it is the version of you that made mistakes, held onto regret, or felt trapped in cycles of self-doubt. Alternatively, this letter may be directed toward another person—someone whose presence, actions, or words have left a lasting imprint on your soul. It could be a former friend, a family member, a partner, or even someone who hurt you in ways you find difficult to put into words.

Once you have chosen who or what to address, allow yourself to write freely. If you are speaking to a past version of yourself, acknowledge your journey with compassion. Let that version of you know they were doing the best they could with the knowledge and emotional capacity they had at the time. Reassure them that they are forgiven, that they are loved, and that their struggles have shaped the growth you experience today. Thank them for their resilience, but also let them know they no longer have to hold onto the pain that accompanied that chapter of your life.

If your letter is addressed to another person, be completely honest. Express the words that were left unsaid—the pain, the disappointment, the anger, or even the gratitude for lessons learned. Release any expectations of how they would respond or whether they would understand. This is not about them; this is about your healing. If you feel resentment, acknowledge it. If you feel sorrow, let yourself grieve. If you feel a mix of emotions, know that healing is rarely linear. Whatever comes up, write it down without judgment.

When you feel you have said everything that needs to be said, pause. Close your eyes and take a deep breath. Notice how your body feels. Do you feel lighter? More vulnerable? Relieved? Emotional? There is no right or wrong way to feel—what matters is that you are giving yourself the space to process and release.

Now, consider how you would like to symbolically let go of this letter. You may choose to burn it (safely), watching the words turn to ash as a representation of release. You might tear it into pieces, flushing away the fragments of what no longer serves you. Perhaps you prefer to bury it, returning the energy to the earth with the intention of transformation. If you'd rather keep it, close your journal with a clear statement of intention, such as: "I release the weight of these words. They no longer hold power over me. I am free."

As a final step, take a few moments to sit in gratitude. Gratitude for the strength it took to face what was buried. Gratitude for the space you are creating within yourself. Gratitude for the journey of healing and renewal that continues each day. You are no longer carrying the past in the same way. You are stepping into a lighter, freer version of yourself.

# Cleansing the Mind for Spiritual Clarity

*"Clear the mind, and the soul will speak."*

**Understanding Mental Detox:**

The mind is a powerful force that shapes the way we experience reality. Every thought, belief, and perception influences not only our emotions but also our spiritual energy. When the mind is cluttered with negativity, fear, and self-doubt, it creates barriers that block clarity, inner peace, and connection to higher consciousness. Just as physical detox removes toxins from the body, mental detox is essential for cleansing the mind of limiting patterns and intrusive thoughts that weigh it down.

Our thoughts are not just fleeting ideas; they are the foundation upon which our lives are built. If the mind is clouded with worry, overthinking, or resentment, it distorts perception, making it difficult to see the truth of a situation. A mind filled with negativity perceives obstacles everywhere, while a mind that has been cleansed and re-centered recognizes opportunities, solutions, and possibilities. By detoxing the mind, we allow space for clarity, deeper self-awareness, and a renewed sense of purpose.

Mental clutter often accumulates over time, unnoticed. It is formed through unresolved emotions, the influence of past experiences, societal conditioning, and even external stimuli like social media, news, and the energy of those around us.

Just as a cluttered room can feel overwhelming and disorganized, a cluttered mind creates stress, anxiety, and emotional exhaustion. A mental detox is the process of decluttering internal chaos, removing toxic thought patterns, and shifting into a state of mental balance and peace.

One of the first steps in this process is recognizing how thoughts shape emotions and behaviors. Negative thinking patterns create a cycle that reinforces stress and unhappiness. When thoughts are repetitive, self-defeating, or overly critical, they manifest as doubt, fear, or resistance, making it harder to trust intuition or embrace personal growth. These mental barriers can cause spiritual stagnation, preventing deeper awareness and alignment with higher self-energy.

A mental detox does not mean ignoring or suppressing negative thoughts. Instead, it involves observing them without attachment, questioning their validity, and replacing them with healthier perspectives. By doing so, we clear the fog that distorts reality and create space for more constructive, uplifting, and spiritually aligned thoughts. This process allows the mind to return to a state of clarity, where intuition becomes stronger, decision-making improves, and inner peace is restored.

When the mind is free from clutter, it becomes a powerful tool for manifestation, mindfulness, and self-discovery. In this journey of spiritual detox, cleansing the mind is essential, as it lays the foundation for deeper emotional healing, greater self-acceptance, and a heightened connection to the present moment. Through intentional practices, reflection, and awareness, the mind can be rewired to embrace positivity, truth, and spiritual clarity, creating a space where inner wisdom can flourish.

**The Power of Mindfulness:**

In a world that constantly pulls attention in multiple directions, the ability to remain present is both a skill and a necessity. The mind is naturally inclined to wander—dwelling on the past, anticipating the future, or getting caught in an endless loop of analysis and self-judgment. This tendency, if left unchecked, leads to overthinking, stress, and a disconnect from the present moment. The weight of excessive thoughts can feel suffocating, leaving little room for clarity or peace. When the mind is clouded with worries, regrets, or an endless stream of "what-ifs," spiritual growth becomes difficult because there is no space for stillness, reflection, or deeper awareness. Mindfulness serves as a powerful antidote to this mental chaos, offering a way to anchor awareness in the now, where true peace and clarity reside.

Mindfulness is more than just a relaxation technique or a temporary escape from daily stress—it is a way of life, a conscious decision to engage fully with each moment rather than being lost in distractions. It is the art of witnessing thoughts as they arise without getting caught up in them, observing emotions without judgment, and experiencing the world as it is rather than through the distorted lens of fear, assumptions, or expectations. In a state of mindfulness, life slows down, allowing the richness of each experience to be fully absorbed rather than rushed through.

Overthinking often arises from the mind's relentless attempt to seek control, certainty, or solutions to problems that may not even exist. The more the mind attempts to analyze, predict, or replay past events, the more tangled it becomes in an endless cycle of thought. This mental overactivity creates stress, anxiety, and even exhaustion, as the brain becomes overworked, processing far more information than necessary. Mindfulness does not aim to suppress thoughts but rather to bring awareness to them without attachment, creating space between the observer and the thoughts themselves. In this space, clarity emerges, and the mental fog begins to lift.

One of the most effective mindfulness techniques is breath awareness. The breath is a direct link between the body and the mind, a constant and rhythmic force that remains present regardless of external circumstances. Unlike thoughts, which fluctuate and shift rapidly, the breath is steady, reliable, and always available as an anchor to bring awareness back to the present moment. Simply focusing on each inhale and exhale can immediately shift attention away from intrusive thoughts, grounding energy and promoting calmness. This simple yet profound practice can be done anywhere, at any time—whether in the middle of a stressful situation, during moments of uncertainty, or even in daily routines when the mind begins to wander. By continuously returning to the breath, mindfulness becomes second nature, a habit that gently trains the mind to let go of unnecessary mental clutter.

Another deeply transformative mindfulness practice is body scanning. This technique involves directing awareness to different parts of the body, observing physical sensations, and consciously releasing tension. Many emotions, especially stress, anxiety, and unresolved trauma, manifest physically—tightness in the shoulders, a clenched jaw, a heavy chest, or even digestive discomfort. The body often speaks before the mind does, storing unresolved emotions in ways that influence overall well-being. By scanning the body with mindful awareness, tension and blockages can be identified and released, allowing a greater sense of ease and connection with the present moment. This technique is particularly powerful when combined with deep breathing, as each exhale serves as an opportunity to let go of tension and reset the nervous system.

Mindful observation is another way to cultivate presence, strengthening the ability to fully engage with the world rather than being lost in thought. This practice can be as simple as watching the movement of leaves in the wind, feeling the warmth of the sun against the skin, listening to the sound of rain, or fully savoring the taste of a meal. Instead of merely existing on autopilot, mindfulness invites full immersion in each experience, making even the simplest moments feel profound and meaningful. The more one engages in this practice, the more life itself begins to feel richer and more vibrant, as awareness deepens and previously overlooked details become sources of beauty and appreciation.

Reducing overthinking requires a conscious effort to step back from thoughts rather than becoming entangled in them. Instead of identifying with every thought that arises, mindfulness teaches the ability to observe them as passing clouds in the sky—temporary, ever-changing, and ultimately separate from the true self. This shift in perspective prevents unnecessary suffering caused by over-identification with thoughts, replacing mental struggle with a sense of peace and detachment. By practicing this awareness regularly, thoughts lose their grip, and the mind becomes less reactive, more stable, and more open to spiritual clarity.

Cultivating inner peace through mindfulness does not mean eliminating all thoughts or emotions; rather, it is about learning to coexist with them without being controlled by them. The mind will always produce thoughts, just as the heart beats and the lungs breathe. The key is not to resist this natural process but to approach it with awareness and acceptance. Instead of being swept away by thoughts, mindfulness offers the ability to gently redirect attention, creating a sense of stillness even in the midst of mental noise.

When mindfulness becomes a daily practice, it transforms the mind into a place of stillness, clarity, and presence. No longer consumed by worries about the future or regrets about the past, the mind begins to rest in the now, where true peace is found. Over time, this shift brings not only mental ease but also a profound spiritual awareness. In this state, intuition sharpens, wisdom deepens, and a sense of alignment with the universe emerges. The more mindfulness is practiced, the more natural it becomes, eventually evolving into a way of being rather than just a technique. And as the mind clears, the soul finds the space to expand, free from the weight of mental clutter, fully present in the beauty of existence.

**Reprogramming Negative Thoughts**

The mind is a powerful force, constantly absorbing, processing, and interpreting information. However, much of what it operates on is shaped by past experiences, deeply ingrained beliefs, and subconscious conditioning. Negative thought patterns often originate from early life experiences, societal influences, or repeated exposure to limiting beliefs. These thoughts may manifest as self-doubt, fear, unworthiness, or an ongoing cycle of internal criticism. When left unchecked, they become automatic, reinforcing themselves through neural pathways that strengthen over time, making negativity feel like an unavoidable truth rather than a mental habit that can be changed.

Reprogramming the mind is not about ignoring or suppressing negative thoughts—it is about recognizing them, understanding their origins, and actively choosing to shift them. Through intentional practice, the brain can be rewired, creating new neural connections that support positive thinking, resilience, and emotional balance. This ability, known as neuroplasticity, proves that thoughts are not fixed but malleable, capable of transformation through conscious effort.

Affirmations are one of the most effective tools for reshaping thought patterns. These are positive statements that reinforce a desired belief or mindset, replacing old, limiting thoughts with new, empowering ones. When repeated consistently, affirmations begin to influence the subconscious, gradually altering how one perceives themselves and the world. However, for affirmations to be effective, they must be believable and emotionally resonant. Simply repeating "I am confident" when deep-seated insecurity exists may feel hollow at first, but pairing affirmations with small, tangible actions that reinforce them makes the shift more authentic. Instead of forcing an unrealistic belief, one might start with "I am learning to trust myself more each day," gradually working toward deeper confidence.

Beyond affirmations, cognitive restructuring is another powerful method for breaking negative thought cycles. This technique, rooted in cognitive-behavioral therapy (CBT), involves identifying irrational or unhelpful thoughts and replacing them with balanced, constructive ones. The first step is awareness—recognizing when a negative thought arises and examining its validity. Often, automatic negative thoughts are exaggerated or distorted. For instance, if a mistake is made, the mind might immediately conclude, "I'm a failure." Cognitive restructuring challenges this by asking, "Is that really true? Does making a mistake define my entire worth?" By breaking down these rigid, self-defeating beliefs, space is created for new perspectives that are more compassionate and realistic.

Visualization is another method that helps reprogram the mind by engaging both thought and emotion. The brain responds to imagined experiences similarly to real ones, meaning that visualizing a desired mindset or outcome can strengthen the neural pathways associated with it. Taking a few moments each day to mentally picture oneself embodying confidence, resilience, or inner peace can reinforce these states as familiar and achievable. When visualization is combined with affirmations and intentional action, the transformation becomes even more profound.

Journaling also plays a significant role in rewiring thought patterns. Writing out negative beliefs and then actively reframing them on paper can create a sense of distance from their influence. This practice allows for deeper self-reflection, uncovering hidden narratives that may have been unconsciously shaping behavior. It also provides an opportunity to track progress, witnessing how thoughts evolve over time with consistent effort.

It's important to acknowledge that reprogramming the mind is not an instant process. The neural pathways that sustain negative thinking have often been reinforced over years, even decades. Changing them requires patience, consistency, and self-compassion. Some days, progress will be evident, while others may feel like setbacks. However, the key is persistence—continuing to redirect thoughts each time negativity arises, knowing that with time, new mental habits will solidify.

As the mind shifts, so does reality. Thoughts shape emotions, which influence actions, which ultimately create one's experience of life. By consciously choosing to reprogram negative thought patterns, an internal transformation occurs—one that extends beyond mental well-being into spiritual clarity, emotional balance, and a deeper sense of self-awareness. Through affirmations, cognitive restructuring, visualization, and journaling, the mind becomes a tool for empowerment rather than limitation, allowing one to move forward with greater freedom, confidence, and peace.

**Guided Meditation:**

A restless mind is like a stormy sea—waves of thoughts crash against each other, pulling attention in countless directions. Without awareness, the mind clings to these thoughts, turning fleeting worries into burdens and small distractions into overwhelming noise. This constant internal dialogue creates a sense of tension and unease, leaving little room for peace. The mind becomes entangled in cycles of overanalyzing the past and anticipating the future, preventing true presence in the moment. Over time, this mental clutter builds up, leading to stress, anxiety, and emotional exhaustion.

Observing thoughts without attachment is a practice that allows space between the self and the mind's endless chatter. It is not about suppressing thoughts or forcing the mind into silence but rather witnessing them without judgment, like clouds drifting across the sky. This practice is a core component of mindfulness and meditation, helping to cultivate a state of awareness where thoughts can arise and pass without control over emotions or actions. The mind naturally generates thoughts—this is its function—but the suffering comes from identifying too closely with them, believing every passing idea or worry to be absolute truth.

The breath becomes an anchor, guiding awareness to the present moment. With each slow inhale and exhale, the body relaxes, releasing tension held in the shoulders, jaw, and hands. The rhythmic rise and fall of the breath creates a steady foundation, grounding the mind when it begins to wander. By focusing on the breath, the present moment becomes more tangible, offering a space of stillness amid the mental noise.

As thoughts begin to surface, they are not to be resisted or engaged with. Instead, they are observed as passing events, much like watching leaves floating down a stream. Some thoughts may be persistent, returning again and again, demanding attention. Others may be subtle, barely forming before they fade. The key is to acknowledge each thought without labeling it as good or bad, right or wrong. Instead of analyzing or judging, the goal is to remain a neutral observer. Every thought is simply energy passing through, and like all things, it will eventually dissipate.

At first, the mind may rebel against this stillness, grasping for distractions or attempting to pull attention away from the present. This is normal. The mind has been conditioned to be in a constant state of movement, always seeking stimulation or resolution. The practice is to gently bring awareness back to the breath each time it drifts. There is no need to feel frustration when thoughts arise— each return to the present moment strengthens the ability to remain centered.

With continued practice, a sense of detachment develops. The mind, once tangled in its own narratives, starts to loosen its grip. Emotional reactions become less automatic, and clarity emerges in the space left behind. Moments of silence may appear between thoughts—brief pauses of pure awareness where the mind is still, yet fully awake. These moments grow longer with practice, revealing a deeper state of presence that is not dependent on external circumstances.

In these moments, the deeper self is felt—an awareness beyond the noise of daily worries and mental habits. A profound realization begins to take shape: thoughts are not reality. They are fleeting, impermanent, and often based on past conditioning rather than present truth. This understanding creates freedom, allowing one to respond to life from a place of wisdom rather than reactivity.

By the end of the meditation, there is a noticeable shift. The mind feels lighter, as if a weight has been lifted. The endless need to chase or push away thoughts diminishes, replaced by a quiet confidence that thoughts do not define reality. There is a newfound ability to witness experiences with greater objectivity, reducing emotional turmoil and increasing inner stability. When the eyes open, the world appears the same, yet something within has changed. There is a renewed sense of clarity and calmness, an awareness that carries forward into daily life, no longer swept away by every passing mental storm.

**Journaling Exercise**

Set aside a quiet moment and reflect on the thoughts that surface repeatedly in your daily life. These may be whispers of self-doubt, harsh judgments, or fears that seem to cycle endlessly. Without filtering or analyzing, write them down exactly as they appear in your mind. Pay attention to patterns—are there specific themes that keep emerging? Do these thoughts arise in particular situations or in response to certain emotions? Acknowledge them without resistance, simply observing their presence on the page. This process is not about judging yourself for having these thoughts but about bringing them into awareness. Often, the most deeply ingrained patterns operate unnoticed in the background, influencing emotions, behaviors, and even physical well-being. By writing them down, you take the first step in loosening their hold over you.

Once you have identified these recurring negative thoughts, take a step back and question their validity. Are they absolute truths, or are they conditioned beliefs shaped by past experiences, societal expectations, or external influences? Challenge their authority over you. Many of the limiting beliefs people hold stem from childhood experiences, moments of rejection, or cultural conditioning that repeatedly reinforced a certain idea. Ask yourself: Would I say this to a friend? Would I believe this about someone else? If not, why am I so willing to believe it about myself? Recognizing that these thoughts are not universal truths but rather conditioned narratives is a powerful realization.

Then, for each negative thought, rewrite it in a way that empowers and uplifts you. If your mind frequently tells you, "I always fail," counter it with, "Every challenge helps me grow and improve." If there is an underlying belief of, "I am not enough," replace it with, "I am constantly evolving and worthy as I am." Choose affirmations that resonate with you deeply, words that feel believable and encouraging rather than forced. The goal is not blind positivity but a genuine shift in perspective—one that acknowledges your struggles while also opening the door for transformation.

Writing these affirmations is only the beginning—let them become a part of your daily practice. Speak them aloud, repeat them in moments of doubt, or place them somewhere visible as gentle reminders. The subconscious mind absorbs repeated statements over time, gradually replacing old narratives with new, healthier ones. You may even choose to incorporate these affirmations into meditation or breathing exercises, reinforcing them with deep, intentional breaths. The more these new, empowering statements are reinforced, the more they begin to reshape internal dialogue, allowing the mind to move from self-limitation to self-acceptance and clarity.

# Emotional Healing and Spiritual Renewal

*"Healing doesn't mean the damage never existed. It means the wounds no longer control your life."*

**How Emotions Store in the Body:**

Emotions are not just fleeting thoughts or reactions; they are energy that becomes embedded in the body. Every experience, every heartbreak, and every unresolved conflict leaves an imprint, shaping not only our mental well-being but also our physical health. The body acts as a vessel for these emotions, storing them in muscles, organs, and even the nervous system. When emotions are not fully processed, they linger beneath the surface, creating tension, discomfort, or even chronic pain.

The mind-body connection is a profound and often underestimated force. Science has shown that stress and emotional suppression can weaken the immune system, increase inflammation, and contribute to various illnesses. Ancient traditions have long understood this, recognizing that emotions like grief, anger, or fear can settle into different parts of the body. For instance, unexpressed sadness may create tightness in the chest, while anger often manifests as tension in the shoulders or jaw. Fear, when deeply rooted, can be felt in the stomach, causing digestive issues or a lingering sense of unease.

Trauma, in particular, leaves a lasting imprint, sometimes without conscious awareness. The body remembers even when the mind has tried to forget. This is why certain situations, words, or even scents can trigger intense emotional responses—it is the body's way of signaling that something remains unresolved. The subconscious mind does not distinguish between past and present; it only reacts. A painful memory stored in the body can cause a person to relive the emotional weight of the original event, even years later.

Releasing these stored emotions requires awareness and intentional healing. It is not enough to intellectually understand emotions; they must be felt and processed. Practices such as breathwork, movement, and deep reflection can help bring buried emotions to the surface, allowing them to be acknowledged and finally released. When emotions are no longer suppressed, they lose their hold, and the body regains its natural state of balance.

Healing on this level creates profound change. By letting go of old emotional baggage, there is a renewed sense of lightness and clarity. The body feels more energized, the mind becomes sharper, and the spirit is no longer weighed down by the past. True healing does not come from avoidance but from allowing oneself to fully experience, express, and release what has been held inside for too long.

**Releasing Emotional Blockages**

Emotional blockages act like stagnant pools of energy, preventing the natural flow of emotions and leaving a person feeling stuck, weighed down, or disconnected. These blockages often stem from suppressed pain, unresolved grief, unexpressed emotions, or past traumas that have accumulated over time. When emotions are not fully processed, they don't simply fade away—they settle into the body, shaping thought patterns, behaviors, and even physical well-being. Over time, these stored emotions create inner resistance, making it difficult to move forward, fully embrace joy, or experience deep inner peace. To restore balance, these emotions need to be consciously released, allowing space for healing and renewal.

One of the most powerful ways to release emotional blockages is through breathwork. The breath is directly connected to the nervous system, and conscious breathing techniques can help regulate emotions, release trapped energy, and bring deep emotional clarity. Shallow breathing, which is common when experiencing stress or emotional pain, reinforces tension in the body and mind. In contrast, intentional breathing techniques, such as diaphragmatic breathing, alternate nostril breathing, or deep rhythmic breaths, activate the parasympathetic nervous system, shifting the body from a state of stress to a state of relaxation. As the breath deepens, it creates a safe space for emotions to surface, sometimes bringing long-buried feelings into awareness. Tears, tingling sensations, or even a sense of lightness often accompany this process, signaling that something is finally being let go.

One particularly effective breathwork technique is the "4-7-8 method," in which you inhale deeply for four seconds, hold the breath for seven seconds, and then exhale slowly for eight seconds. This pattern not only calms the nervous system but also encourages deep emotional release. Another technique, known as "connected breathing," involves continuous inhales and exhales without pausing in between, which can bring repressed emotions to the surface in a powerful way. Many who practice breathwork for emotional release report experiencing vivid memories, unexpected emotional breakthroughs, or even a sense of euphoria as the body unburdens itself from stored emotional energy.

Movement is another powerful tool for emotional release. Unprocessed emotions tend to settle in different areas of the body, creating tension, stiffness, or even pain.

Physical movement—whether through yoga, stretching, or intuitive dance—helps break up this stagnant energy and encourages the body to release stored emotions. Certain postures and stretches, especially those targeting the hips, shoulders, and chest, can unlock deeply held emotional patterns. The hips, for example, are known to store unresolved emotions such as fear, grief, and past trauma. Many people find that deep hip-opening stretches, like pigeon pose in yoga, trigger emotional responses, sometimes bringing tears or a sense of emotional relief.

Intuitive movement, which involves allowing the body to move freely in a way that feels natural, can be just as effective. Dancing, shaking, or even swaying gently to music allows emotions to be expressed and released rather than repressed. The key is to move without overthinking—letting the body lead the way. When combined with mindful breathing, movement becomes a form of active healing, allowing emotions to surface, be witnessed, and then flow out of the body.

Sound therapy works on an even deeper vibrational level, tapping into the energetic body to dissolve emotional blockages. Sound carries frequency, and different frequencies resonate with different emotional states.

Singing bowls, chanting, humming, or even listening to specific frequencies such as solfeggio tones can help shift emotions and bring a sense of inner harmony. The vibrations work beyond the conscious mind, helping to clear dense energy and bring about emotional balance. Simply humming or toning sounds, especially from the throat, can release emotions that may have been stuck in the body for years.

One effective practice is vocal toning, in which you produce a long, sustained sound, such as an "Ahhh" or "Ommm," allowing the vibrations to resonate through your chest and throat. This practice is particularly beneficial for clearing blockages related to suppressed communication, unspoken emotions, or repressed truths. Similarly, listening to binaural beats or Tibetan singing bowls while meditating can facilitate deep emotional release by shifting brainwave activity into a state of relaxation and introspection.

Each of these techniques works differently for each person, and the key is finding what resonates most. Some may feel an immediate sense of relief, while others may need to practice consistently before noticing deep shifts. Emotional detox is not about forcing emotions to leave but rather creating a safe and supportive environment where they can naturally dissolve. When emotions are no longer trapped, the heart feels lighter, the mind becomes clearer, and the spirit is free to expand into a state of greater peace and presence.

Letting go of stored emotions is a process, not a single event. There may be days when emotions surface unexpectedly, and others when everything feels light and effortless. The journey of emotional healing requires patience and self-compassion. By consistently practicing breathwork, movement, and sound therapy, the process of release becomes easier, and over time, old wounds begin to heal. As emotional blockages dissolve, energy flows more freely, leading to greater clarity, creativity, and a deeper connection to oneself and the world.

**Healing the Inner Child**

Within each of us lives an inner child—a part of our subconscious mind that holds memories, emotions, and experiences from our early years. This inner child carries both the joy and wonder of youth as well as the wounds inflicted by unmet needs, abandonment, rejection, or emotional neglect. The wounds of the inner child do not simply remain in the past; they weave themselves into the fabric of adult emotions, relationships, and perceptions of self-worth. Without conscious healing, these wounds can manifest as deep-seated insecurities, fears of abandonment, difficulty setting boundaries, people-pleasing tendencies, or patterns of self-sabotage.

Healing the inner child is not about blaming the past but rather acknowledging what was lost, neglected, or wounded and offering that part of yourself the love, safety, and validation it needed then—and still needs now. This process allows for emotional liberation, deeper self-awareness, and the ability to break unhealthy patterns that no longer serve your highest good.

To begin, it is essential to recognize how inner child wounds shape your present experiences. Certain triggers in adulthood—such as rejection, criticism, or feelings of being ignored—may evoke emotions that seem disproportionate to the situation. These intense reactions often stem from childhood wounds that were never fully processed. For example, if a child grew up feeling that their emotions were invalidated or dismissed, they may develop an unconscious belief that their feelings do not matter. As an adult, they may struggle with expressing needs, fearing that they will be ignored or ridiculed. Similarly, someone who experienced abandonment in childhood may develop deep-seated anxiety in relationships, fearing that people will leave them at any moment.

One of the most effective ways to heal the inner child is through reparenting—a process of offering yourself the love, care, and support that you may not have received as a child. This involves recognizing what your younger self needed and actively providing it in the present moment. It could mean speaking to yourself with kindness rather than criticism, honoring your emotions instead of suppressing them, or creating a sense of safety within rather than seeking it externally. Reparenting is a gradual process, requiring patience and deep self-compassion.

Visualization is a powerful tool in inner child healing. Imagine meeting your younger self at a specific age when you felt wounded or neglected. Picture them standing before you—how do they look? What emotions are they carrying? What do they need to hear? As you visualize this, speak to your inner child with love and reassurance, letting them know that they are safe, worthy, and deeply loved. This simple practice can begin to mend old wounds, bringing comfort to the parts of yourself that have long been yearning for acknowledgment.

Another method of inner child healing is engaging in activities that once brought you joy as a child. Often, as adults, we become disconnected from the simple pleasures that once lit up our spirits—drawing, playing, singing, exploring nature, or even allowing ourselves to be silly without fear of judgment. These activities rekindle the innocence and creativity of childhood, reminding us of the joy and freedom that still exist within. The more you nurture your inner child, the more your spirit feels lighter, and the emotional weight of the past begins to dissolve.

Journaling is also an incredibly effective tool in inner child work. Writing a letter to your younger self—offering the words of comfort and encouragement you needed back then—can be a profound exercise in emotional healing. Allow yourself to express any emotions that arise, whether it be grief, anger, or deep longing. You can also write from the perspective of your inner child, letting them express their fears, sadness, or unmet needs. Through this dialogue, healing begins as the inner child finally feels heard and seen.

Ultimately, healing the inner child is a journey of self-acceptance and emotional renewal. It is about creating a nurturing relationship with yourself—one built on love, trust, and gentleness. As you integrate your inner child's wounds with compassion, you free yourself from the burdens of the past, allowing your heart to open, your emotions to flow freely, and your spirit to embrace life with a renewed sense of peace and wholeness.

**Guided Meditation**

Close your eyes and take a deep, slow breath in. As you exhale, allow any tension in your body to melt away. With each breath, feel yourself becoming lighter, as though a soft wave of warmth is washing over you, releasing all worries, stress, and distractions.

Now, imagine yourself walking through a peaceful, serene landscape. It might be a sunlit forest, a quiet beach, or a vast open meadow—wherever you feel most at ease. The air is fresh, and the atmosphere carries a deep sense of safety and warmth. As you walk, notice the gentle sounds around you—the rustling of leaves, the distant song of birds, or the soft whisper of the wind.

Up ahead, you see a small child sitting alone. As you approach, you begin to recognize this child—it is you, at a younger age. Take a moment to observe them. How old are they? What expression is on their face? Are they playing, waiting, or perhaps looking hesitant or sad? Notice their energy, their posture, and their emotions.

Gently, without rushing, move closer and sit beside them. If they are open to it, greet them with kindness. Let them know you are here for them. This is your inner child—the part of you that has carried both the joys and wounds of your past. Take a moment to feel their presence.

Now, speak to them with love and understanding. You may say, I see you. I hear you. You are safe with me. I love you just as you are. Let your words be soft and reassuring. If your inner child looks sad, ask them what they need. Do they need to feel protected? Do they need to be held? Do they need to hear words of encouragement? Allow them to express whatever emotions arise. Be patient, and let them know they are no longer alone.

If there is any pain, fear, or sadness they have been holding onto, gently invite them to release it. You may visualize a warm golden light surrounding both of you—a light of pure love and healing. As it glows brighter, imagine this light dissolving any old fears, wounds, or feelings of abandonment. See your inner child's face softening, their body relaxing, and their energy becoming lighter.

If you feel ready, embrace them. Hold them in your arms and let them feel the warmth of your unconditional love. Whisper to them, You are safe. You are loved. You are enough. Stay in this moment for as long as you need, absorbing the deep connection between your present self and your younger self.

When you feel complete, let your inner child know that they are always with you and that you will continue to care for them. Whenever they need comfort, you will listen. Whenever they need love, you will provide it. As you prepare to leave, watch as they smile, feeling lighter, freer, and deeply loved.

Slowly, bring your awareness back to the present moment. Feel your breath moving in and out. Gently wiggle your fingers and toes, and when you are ready, open your eyes. Carry this warmth with you, knowing that the connection to your inner child has been strengthened, and healing has begun.

### Journaling Exercise

Writing to your younger self is a powerful act of healing, love, and reassurance. It allows you to bridge the gap between who you were and who you have become, offering the wisdom, kindness, and comfort that your younger self may have longed for. This exercise is not just about looking back; it's about releasing old wounds, embracing growth, and acknowledging the strength you have carried through every phase of your journey.

Find a quiet space where you won't be interrupted. Set the intention to write from the heart, without judgment or hesitation. Take a few deep breaths, centering yourself in the present moment. When you're ready, close your eyes and visualize your younger self. You may picture a specific age—a child, a teenager, or even a version of yourself from just a few years ago. See them in detail: what they're wearing, the expression on their face, and the emotions they carry. Do they look happy, hopeful, scared, or lonely? What do they need to hear?

Now, begin your letter. Start by addressing them lovingly, using a name or term that feels natural to you.

"Dear younger me, I see you. I remember you. And I want you to know that you are not alone."

Write as if you are sitting beside them, holding their hand, offering them the support and understanding they may have lacked at the time. Acknowledge their struggles with empathy:

"I know how hard things feel right now. I know you are carrying so much—uncertainty, fear, sadness, or doubt. But I want you to know that you are stronger than you realize, and everything you are facing will shape you into the incredible person you are meant to be."

Offer them the love they deserve, the encouragement they may have needed, and the forgiveness for any guilt or self-blame they have held onto:

"You are worthy of love, just as you are. You don't have to be perfect, and you don't have to carry everything alone. I forgive you for the moments you thought you weren't enough. I forgive you for the times you were hard on yourself. And I want you to know that everything will be okay."

You might also want to remind them of the beauty they hold within and how their journey unfolds into something greater than they ever imagined:

"One day, you will look back and realize how far you've come. You will find happiness, love, and purpose in ways you never expected. You will heal. And you will become someone who loves and accepts themselves fully."

Close the letter with warmth and reassurance, promising to always be there for them:

"I will carry you with me always. Whenever you feel lost, just know that I am here, and I love you. You are safe. You are enough. And you are deeply, unconditionally loved."

When you finish, take a moment to reflect on how you feel. You may experience a sense of release, peace, or even emotions you didn't expect. If it feels right, you can read the letter aloud to yourself, as if speaking directly to the younger version of you. Some people find comfort in keeping their letter, while others choose to burn it as a symbolic act of letting go.

This exercise is an act of self-compassion and emotional renewal. It reminds you that healing is not about erasing the past but about embracing and loving every part of your journey—including the parts of you that once felt lost.

# Detoxing Your Environment for Spiritual Growth

*"Your environment is a reflection of your energy—clear the space, and your spirit will breathe freely."*

**Your Space, Your Energy**

The spaces we inhabit hold energy, shaping our emotions, thoughts, and overall well-being. Our homes, workplaces, and even digital environments are reflections of our inner state, and just as clutter accumulates externally, energetic stagnation can build up internally. When we live in a space filled with disorder—whether it's physical mess, digital distractions, or emotionally draining atmospheres—it creates unseen barriers that block spiritual clarity and growth. Every object carries an imprint of the past, every digital notification fragments attention, and every toxic environment drains the soul in ways we might not immediately recognize.

Physical clutter is more than just an inconvenience; it has a direct impact on mental and spiritual energy. Walking into a disorganized room can induce feelings of stress, overwhelm, and mental fatigue. When every surface is covered in items that serve no purpose, when closets overflow with things we no longer need, and when we surround ourselves with objects tied to outdated identities, the weight of the past lingers. Spiritual growth requires space—space for new energy, new experiences, and new perspectives. By decluttering our physical surroundings, we signal to the universe that we are ready to release what no longer serves us and invite in clarity and renewal.

Just as physical spaces can hold stagnant energy, digital spaces can become overwhelming and mentally exhausting. The constant influx of information, endless scrolling, and exposure to negativity on social media can subtly erode inner peace. Every unread email, every overwhelming notification, and every comparison-based post adds invisible clutter to the mind. Detoxing from digital distractions doesn't mean complete disconnection, but rather creating a mindful relationship with technology. Setting boundaries, curating content that nourishes rather than depletes, and making space for moments of silence are crucial for maintaining spiritual balance in a world that constantly demands attention.

Beyond physical and digital clutter, the environments we immerse ourselves in—our homes, workplaces, and social circles—play a significant role in our energetic well-being. Some spaces feel heavy the moment we enter them, weighed down by unresolved tension, conflict, or negativity. These spaces carry the residual energy of past events, emotions, and interactions. In contrast, environments infused with warmth, love, and intentionality uplift the spirit and provide a sanctuary for healing and growth. Being mindful of where we spend our time, who we share our energy with, and how we cultivate our personal space is a vital part of spiritual detox.

When we cleanse our surroundings, we are not just tidying up—we are making room for transformation. A home free of clutter becomes a temple for peace, a digital space free of toxicity fosters mindfulness, and a social environment free of negativity allows spiritual expansion. Every small step toward detoxing our surroundings is a step toward a clearer, lighter, and more harmonious existence.

**Cleansing Rituals**

Cleansing rituals are powerful tools for shifting energy, promoting clarity, and creating a space that nurtures spiritual well-being. Throughout history, different cultures have developed unique purification methods to remove stagnant or negative energy and invite in positive vibrations. These practices, rooted in both ancient wisdom and modern spiritual traditions, serve as a way to restore balance within one's surroundings and within the self. Whether performed daily, weekly, or during times of emotional heaviness, cleansing rituals help release energetic blockages, making way for renewed vitality and inner peace.

One of the most widely recognized cleansing rituals is smudging, an ancient practice that involves burning sacred herbs to purify a space, object, or person. Sage, particularly white sage, is a common herb used for smudging due to its strong purification properties. As the dried leaves burn, the rising smoke is believed to absorb and transmute negative energy, leaving behind an atmosphere of clarity and peace. Indigenous cultures have long used smudging in ceremonies, rituals, and daily practices, viewing it as a way to connect with the spirit world while clearing away unwanted energies. Palo santo, another revered cleansing tool, comes from a tree native to South America and carries a distinct, grounding aroma that helps remove negativity and enhance spiritual connection. When smudging, it is essential to set an intention—whether it be releasing stress, clearing out old energy, or inviting in fresh opportunities—since intention directs the energy and amplifies the ritual's effectiveness.

Beyond smoke cleansing, water is an equally potent medium for energetic purification. Salt baths have been used for centuries as a means of physical and spiritual detoxification. Salt, particularly sea salt, Epsom salt, and Himalayan salt, has the ability to draw out negative energy, release tension, and restore a sense of calm.

Immersing in a warm salt bath not only soothes the muscles but also cleanses the aura, dissolving emotional heaviness that may have built up over time. For those who prefer an alternative, a simple salt scrub in the shower can achieve similar effects by exfoliating both the skin and energetic residue. To deepen the cleansing process, adding essential oils such as lavender, rosemary, or eucalyptus can enhance relaxation and further clear stagnant energy.

Crystals also play a significant role in purifying and protecting energy. Certain stones, such as black tourmaline, selenite, and clear quartz, are particularly effective in absorbing negativity and maintaining an energetically clean environment. Black tourmaline is known for its grounding and protective qualities, acting as a shield against external influences. Selenite, often referred to as a "liquid light" crystal, has the ability to cleanse and recharge other stones while promoting spiritual clarity. Placing selenite wands near windows, doorways, or under pillows can help keep energy flowing freely. Clear quartz, often called the "master healer," amplifies intention and can be programmed for purification purposes. Holding these crystals during meditation, carrying them throughout the day, or placing them strategically around a home can create a continuous cleansing effect, reinforcing a sense of balance and harmony.

Another effective way to clear energy is through sound healing. Sound has a profound impact on vibrational frequency, and certain tones can break up stagnant or heavy energy in a space. Tibetan singing bowls, crystal bowls, bells, and chimes are commonly used to shift energy through sound waves. Clapping hands in the corners of a room, ringing a bell, or playing high-frequency music can help disperse dense energy and invite in a sense of renewal. Chanting mantras, such as "Om" or other sacred sounds, also elevates the energetic field, promoting spiritual alignment.

In addition to these traditional practices, environmental factors play a significant role in maintaining an energetically balanced space. Fresh air and sunlight are natural cleansers, helping to uplift and revitalize a room's energy. Opening windows, allowing natural light to enter, and introducing plants into the environment can create a space that supports spiritual and emotional well-being. Plants like sage, aloe vera, and lavender not only purify the air but also bring in a natural sense of harmony.

Regular decluttering—removing unused or broken items—also contributes to a cleaner, lighter atmosphere.

Ultimately, cleansing rituals are not just about the physical actions but about the intention behind them. The more mindfulness and purpose infused into the practice, the more effective it becomes. These rituals serve as reminders that energy is constantly shifting, and just as we cleanse our bodies, minds, and emotions, our surroundings require the same care. By engaging in these practices regularly, we create an environment that fosters spiritual growth, emotional clarity, and a deeper connection with our highest self.

**The Digital Detox**

In today's hyper-connected world, digital stimulation is nearly constant, shaping our thoughts, emotions, and overall well-being. While technology offers numerous benefits, the relentless influx of information, opinions, and distractions can create mental clutter, diminish focus, and weaken our connection to our inner wisdom. A digital detox is not about rejecting technology entirely but about consciously reducing digital noise to regain clarity, balance, and a stronger sense of intuition. By stepping away from the overstimulation of social media, news cycles, and external negativity, we create space for deeper self-awareness, emotional regulation, and spiritual alignment.

Social media, in particular, has a profound impact on mental and emotional states. The curated nature of online platforms often distorts reality, leading to comparisons, self-doubt, and feelings of inadequacy. The endless scrolling through updates, opinions, and advertisements can leave the mind restless, absorbing energy that could otherwise be directed toward self-reflection and personal growth. Many people turn to social media out of habit, seeking validation, entertainment, or distraction from discomfort. However, this habit often results in information overload and emotional fatigue. Taking breaks—even temporarily—allows the nervous system to reset, helping to reduce anxiety, improve focus, and cultivate a more grounded state of being.

Beyond social media, constant exposure to news and external negativity can create a heightened sense of stress and powerlessness. While staying informed is important, excessive consumption of negative or fear-inducing content can lead to chronic worry and emotional exhaustion. The human brain is not designed to process an endless stream of crises, conflicts, and controversies. When bombarded with distressing headlines, the mind shifts into a reactive state, making it difficult to access intuition, creativity, and inner peace. Setting boundaries around news consumption—such as limiting exposure to once or twice a day, choosing balanced sources, or even taking temporary breaks—can significantly improve mental clarity and emotional stability.

Reducing digital noise also allows for a deeper reconnection with intuition. Intuition thrives in stillness. When the mind is constantly occupied with external inputs, the subtle inner voice of wisdom is drowned out. Moments of silence and disconnection from screens create space for self-awareness, reflection, and intuitive insights to emerge. Many people find that when they step away from technology—even for short periods—they experience a greater sense of clarity, inner knowing, and alignment with their true selves.

Practical steps for a digital detox can be customized based on individual needs and lifestyles. Some may benefit from setting specific screen-free hours each day, such as avoiding phones in the morning or before bed. Others may choose designated "unplugged" days, where they intentionally disconnect from social media, emails, and news. Turning off notifications, using apps that track screen time, or setting boundaries—such as keeping devices out of the bedroom—can help cultivate healthier digital habits. Engaging in offline activities such as reading, journaling, nature walks, or meditation can further reinforce the benefits of reducing digital distractions.

Ultimately, a digital detox is about reclaiming mental space, emotional well-being, and spiritual connection. It is an opportunity to shift from external stimulation to internal awareness, allowing intuition to flourish and fostering a deeper, more meaningful relationship with oneself. By consciously reducing digital noise, we create a more harmonious balance between the modern world and our inner wisdom, paving the way for greater clarity, peace, and personal transformation.

**Guided Meditation**

Close your eyes and take a deep breath, feeling the air fill your lungs as you inhale deeply through your nose. Hold for a moment, then exhale slowly, releasing any tension, stress, or negativity. With each breath, allow yourself to sink deeper into relaxation, feeling the weight of your body ease into the surface beneath you. As your breath steadies, picture yourself standing beneath a vast night sky filled with stars. Above you, a soft beam of silver-blue light descends, wrapping around you like a protective cocoon. This is the energy of your Higher Self, luminous and infinite. As you breathe, feel this celestial light gently flowing through you, awakening a deep sense of wisdom and clarity.

With every inhale, silver-blue light, growing brighter and stronger. As it spreads throughout your body, it washes away any lingering heaviness or stagnant energy. Feel it flowing into your arms, down your legs, and up through your head, illuminating every part of you with warmth and peace. This is your protective energy, your natural aura, and as it expands beyond your body, it begins to form a radiant shield around you.

It is strong, resilient, and impenetrable to any negative energy. The light pulsates with every breath, growing brighter with each inhale and solidifying with every exhale. This shield is uniquely yours—its color, texture, and intensity align perfectly with what you need in this moment. It may shimmer like a translucent veil or glow with the steady power of the sun. However it appears to you, trust that this energy is exactly what you need for protection and strength.

As you sit within this shield, begin to sense any outside energies attempting to influence you. Perhaps there are thoughts of doubt or stress, emotions that are not your own, or lingering negativity from your environment. Watch as these energies approach, only to be deflected by your shield. They cannot enter. They cannot disturb your peace. They dissolve upon contact, melting into nothingness, leaving you untouched.

Now, take a moment to strengthen your shield further. With every breath, imagine its light thickening, solidifying, becoming a fortress of protection. If there are any weak spots, direct your breath there, reinforcing those areas until they feel just as strong as the rest of your aura. You are in complete control of your energy, and only love, positivity, and truth may pass through.

Affirm yourself "I am protected. My energy is my own. I set clear and strong boundaries, allowing only love and light into my space. No negativity may enter. I am safe, whole, and empowered."

Sit in this energy for a few moments, basking in the feeling of strength and security. Let the shield settle around you like a second skin, always present, always active. Know that this protective barrier is something you can call upon anytime, anywhere. Whether in a crowded space, a stressful situation, or simply feeling energetically vulnerable, you can return to this meditation, reinforce your shield, and stand firm in your own power.

When you are ready, begin to bring awareness back to your body. Wiggle your fingers and toes, roll your shoulders, and take one final deep breath, inhaling light and exhaling gratitude. Gently open your eyes, feeling refreshed, grounded, and completely protected. Carry this shield with you throughout your day, knowing that your energy is sacred and that you hold the power to keep it strong and unshaken.

### Journaling Exercise

Take a quiet moment to reflect on your surroundings and the people in your life. Grab your journal and begin by describing the physical spaces where you spend the most time—your home, workplace, car, or any other environment that plays a significant role in your daily routine. Pay close attention to how these spaces make you feel on an energetic level. Are there places where you feel at peace, inspired, or rejuvenated? Conversely, are there areas that feel heavy, cluttered, or energetically stagnant?

Describe these spaces in detail. What objects are present? Are there items that carry emotional weight from the past, such as gifts from people you no longer speak to, old belongings tied to painful memories, or clutter that feels overwhelming? Consider whether your space supports your spiritual and emotional well-being or if it adds to your stress and fatigue. If certain areas drain your energy, what small steps could you take to transform them? Perhaps clearing out unnecessary items, bringing in fresh air and natural light, or incorporating elements that evoke comfort and positivity, such as plants, candles, or meaningful artwork.

Now, shift your focus to the people in your life. Think about the individuals you interact with regularly—friends, family members, colleagues, or acquaintances. Begin by listing those who leave you feeling uplifted, energized, and inspired. What qualities do these people have that contribute to their positive energy? Do they listen with compassion, encourage your growth, or share in your joy without judgment? How do you feel in their presence— safe, supported, understood? Write about the moments when you've felt truly seen and valued by these individuals.

Next, turn your attention to the people who seem to drain your energy. These may be individuals who constantly complain, bring negativity into conversations, or project their stress and fears onto you. Do you notice yourself feeling emotionally exhausted, anxious, or even guilty after being around them? Are there certain dynamics where you overextend yourself, suppress your emotions, or walk away feeling depleted? Reflect on any patterns that emerge in these relationships. Are you holding onto connections out of obligation or fear of change?

After writing about these experiences honestly and without guilt, consider what changes you can make to cultivate more supportive environments and relationships. Are there spaces you can declutter, refresh, or avoid altogether? Can you establish boundaries with those who drain you, even if it's just limiting how much time or energy you give to them? What small adjustments can you make to create an atmosphere that nurtures your well-being?

Finally, end this journaling session with a commitment to yourself. Write a few sentences declaring how you intend to create a more nourishing environment—whether it's by surrounding yourself with positivity, setting healthy boundaries, or releasing what no longer serves your highest good. You may also include an affirmation, such as:

"I choose to fill my space and life with energy that uplifts me. I release what drains me and embrace what nourishes my spirit."

Let this exercise serve as a reminder that you have the power to shape your surroundings and relationships in ways that align with your highest well-being.

# Aligning with Your True Self

*"When you strip away the noise of the world, what remains is your true self—waiting to be heard, seen, and fully embraced."*

**What Is Authentic Living**

Authentic living is the process of peeling back the layers of external influence to uncover the truest version of yourself. From the moment we are born, we are shaped by societal norms, familial expectations, and cultural narratives that dictate how we should think, behave, and perceive the world. These influences, though sometimes well-intentioned, can pull us away from our inner essence, leading us to adopt identities that do not truly reflect who we are at our core. We find ourselves making decisions based on what is expected of us rather than what resonates with our soul. This disconnection can manifest as feelings of restlessness, dissatisfaction, or even an underlying sense of emptiness, as if we are living a life scripted by others rather than embracing our own unique path.

True authenticity begins with self-inquiry. It requires an honest evaluation of the beliefs, habits, and desires that govern our daily lives. Are they truly ours, or have they been adopted to conform to external expectations? The journey to authentic living is not about rejecting all societal structures but rather discerning which aspects align with our true nature and which ones hold us back. It is about unlearning what does not serve us and embracing the freedom to define ourselves on our own terms.

Fear is one of the greatest barriers to authenticity. The fear of judgment, rejection, or failure can keep us tethered to a version of ourselves that feels safe but unfulfilling. We hesitate to express our true thoughts, pursue our deepest passions, or live in alignment with our intuition because of the potential consequences. Yet, the cost of denying our authenticity is far greater than the temporary discomfort of stepping into the unknown. When we suppress our true selves, we experience internal conflict, leading to stress, anxiety, and even physical exhaustion. The energy spent maintaining a façade drains us, whereas living in alignment with our truth energizes and empowers us.

Embracing authenticity is a radical act of self-love. It is the decision to honor your desires, trust your intuition, and walk your own path regardless of external opinions. It is understanding that your worth is not defined by how well you fit into societal molds but by the depth of your connection to your own soul. When you step into authenticity, you not only liberate yourself but also inspire others to do the same.

**Uncovering Your Soul's Purpose**

Discovering your soul's purpose is not about finding a single, definitive answer—it is a continuous unfolding, a process of returning to your core essence. In a world that often measures success by external achievements, many people spend their lives chasing accomplishments, only to feel an emptiness they cannot quite name. True purpose is not something to be acquired; it is something to be uncovered, a deep remembering of what has always been within you. This requires self-inquiry, courage, and a willingness to move beyond societal conditioning to embrace the truth of who you are.

The journey to discovering your purpose begins with self-awareness. Often, we are so entangled in obligations and expectations that we forget to ask ourselves the fundamental questions: What makes me feel alive? What activities bring me into a state of flow, where time ceases to exist? What kind of work or creative expression fuels my soul rather than drains it? These questions help peel back the layers of conditioning, guiding you toward what genuinely matters to you—not what you think should matter.

A powerful way to begin this journey is by revisiting childhood passions. Before responsibilities, self-doubt, and societal pressures shaped our paths, we gravitated toward activities and experiences that brought us joy. What did you love to do as a child? What topics fascinated you? What dreams filled your mind before practicality took over?

Often, the things that made us light up as children hold valuable clues to our deeper calling. Though our interests may evolve, the core essence of what makes us feel purposeful often remains the same.

Another key to uncovering your purpose is observing where you naturally offer value to the world. Purpose is often woven into the things we do effortlessly—qualities we take for granted because they feel so natural to us. Ask yourself: What do people consistently seek my advice or help with? What talents or skills do I bring to situations without even thinking about it? When do I feel most aligned with myself, regardless of recognition or reward? Sometimes, the answer is hidden in plain sight.

However, uncovering purpose is not always about what we do—it is about who we are becoming. Society often equates purpose with a career or a specific role, but true alignment is about the energy you bring into the world. Are you someone who inspires, who heals, who teaches, who creates? Purpose is not confined to a title or profession; it is a way of being. This means that even if you do not have a clear, structured vision of your purpose, you can still live with intention by focusing on the values and impact you wish to embody every day.

To deepen this journey, take time to write a personal mission statement. This does not have to be rigid or perfect; it is simply an evolving declaration of what feels most true to you. Answer the following prompts in your journal:

*What are my core values? (Think about principles like honesty, creativity, connection, or growth.)*

*How do I want to contribute to the world? (Through healing, leadership, service, expression?)*

*What brings me the deepest sense of fulfillment, beyond material success?*

*If fear, judgment, and limitations did not exist, what would I pursue wholeheartedly?*

Let your answers flow without overthinking them. Often, the first things that come to mind are the most revealing. Over time, as you revisit these reflections, patterns will emerge, guiding you toward greater clarity.

Tuning into intuition is another key aspect of reconnecting with your purpose. Unlike the analytical mind, which seeks logical explanations and structured paths, intuition speaks in quiet nudges, deep knowing, and persistent curiosity. Pay attention to the things you feel drawn to, even if they do not immediately make sense. Are there activities, places, or topics that keep calling to you? Do you feel an unexplainable pull toward a certain direction? Learning to trust these subtle signals is an essential part of the process. Meditation, stillness, and solitude allow you to quiet external noise and tune into this inner guidance.

It is also important to recognize that purpose evolves. Many people believe they must find one singular life purpose, but in reality, it shifts as we grow. The more we honor our passions, listen to our inner wisdom, and release the fear of living authentically, the more naturally our path unfolds. Purpose is not a fixed destination—it is a way of engaging with life, a commitment to living in alignment with our highest truth.

Ultimately, aligning with your soul's purpose is about liberation. It is about peeling away layers of self-doubt and external conditioning to reveal the vibrant, whole being you have always been. It is about stepping forward with intention, knowing that your existence alone is meaningful. The path is already within you—your only task is to trust it, follow its whispers, and allow it to unfold in its own time.

**Overcoming Fear and Self-Doubt**

Fear and self-doubt are some of the greatest obstacles to personal and spiritual growth. They create invisible barriers that keep you from fully stepping into your true potential, often convincing you that you are not capable, worthy, or ready. These limiting beliefs, deeply ingrained by past experiences, societal pressures, or internalized narratives, shape the way you see yourself and the world. But in truth, fear is only as powerful as the attention and belief you give it. When you begin to question the stories that fear tells you, you take the first step toward reclaiming your power.

Breaking free from limiting beliefs requires awareness, conscious effort, and a willingness to challenge the thoughts that have kept you stuck. The first step is to recognize where these beliefs originate. Were they passed down from family? Rooted in past failures? Reinforced by external voices that doubted you? Once you identify the source, you can begin to dismantle these fears by replacing them with new, empowering perspectives.

Every time you catch yourself thinking, "I can't," ask yourself, "Why not?" Often, the reasons that come up are based on assumptions rather than truths.

Taking action despite fear is one of the most powerful ways to weaken its grip. Fear thrives in inaction—it grows stronger when you avoid challenges and stay within your comfort zone. But when you take even the smallest step forward, you prove to yourself that fear does not control you. Each step builds confidence, creating a momentum that makes future challenges feel less overwhelming. You may not eliminate fear entirely, but you can learn to move forward with it, using it as a guide rather than a barrier.

Self-doubt also diminishes when you cultivate self-trust. Learning to trust yourself means recognizing that you have the strength, resilience, and wisdom to handle whatever comes your way. It means making decisions based on your inner guidance rather than the fear of failure. Developing this trust takes practice—by setting small goals, following through on commitments to yourself, and celebrating even the smallest victories, you reinforce the belief that you are capable.

True spiritual growth happens when you stop waiting to feel "ready" and start believing that you already have everything you need within you. Fear and self-doubt may whisper their doubts, but they do not define you. When you choose to act in alignment with your authentic self despite these doubts, you step into a life that is truly your own.

**Guided Meditation**

Close your eyes and take a slow, deep breath in. Hold it for a moment, feeling your lungs expand fully, then exhale gently, releasing any tension in your body. With each breath, imagine yourself sinking deeper into relaxation, allowing the outside world to fade as you turn your attention inward. Let go of any thoughts or distractions, bringing your awareness fully into the present moment.

Now, visualize yourself standing in an open, serene space bathed in a warm, golden light. This space feels safe, welcoming, and filled with a sense of peace. The air is calm and carries a gentle energy that soothes and uplifts you. As you stand here, take a moment to notice how your body feels. With each inhale, you are drawing in clarity and light; with each exhale, you are releasing doubt, stress, and fear.

In front of you, a soft path stretches forward, glowing with a gentle radiance, guiding you toward a sacred place of wisdom and truth. This path represents your soul's journey, a road that leads you to a deeper understanding of yourself. As you take slow, intentional steps along this path, you feel lighter, as if shedding layers of self-doubt and limitations with each movement. Feel the burdens you have carried—old fears, worries, and external expectations—gently dissolving into the air, disappearing into the light around you.

As you continue walking, you notice a figure in the distance. At first, they appear as a radiant glow, shimmering with warmth and love. As you step closer, the figure begins to take shape. This is your Higher Self—the truest, most authentic version of you, free from fear, free from conditioning, existing in complete alignment with your soul's purpose. Your Higher Self exudes a deep, unwavering confidence, a presence of peace and wisdom that feels both powerful and familiar.

You feel an overwhelming sense of calm and belonging as you come face to face with this divine version of yourself. There is no judgment, no expectation—only pure acceptance and love. Your Higher Self extends a hand toward you, and as you reach out and connect, a warm, soothing energy flows through your body. It moves through your heart, your mind, your spirit—clearing away any remaining doubts and filling you with confidence, strength, and clarity.

Take a moment to fully embrace this connection. Feel the love and guidance radiating from within. Know that you are never alone—this part of you has always been here, always guiding you, even in moments of uncertainty.

Now, in this space of deep connection, ask your Higher Self whatever is on your heart. Perhaps you seek clarity on your life's purpose, guidance on a decision, or reassurance that you are on the right path. Whatever it may be, trust that the answer will come to you in the way that is most natural—through words, images, sensations, or simply a deep inner knowing. Be open to receiving without expectation.

Spend some time here, absorbing the wisdom and love radiating from your Higher Self. Let the answers flow freely, trusting that whatever guidance you receive is exactly what you need in this moment. If nothing comes right away, that is okay too. Sometimes, messages arrive later, when the mind is still and the heart is open.

When you are ready, take a deep breath and express gratitude for this connection. Thank your Higher Self for the guidance, love, and wisdom shared in this moment. Know that this presence is always within you, accessible at any time when you need strength, clarity, or reassurance.

Slowly, begin to return. Visualize yourself walking back along the glowing path, carrying with you the peace and wisdom you have received. With each step, feel yourself becoming more present in your physical body. Take another deep breath, feeling your awareness returning to the here and now. Wiggle your fingers and toes, gently bringing movement back into your body. When you are ready, open your eyes.

Sit for a moment, allowing yourself to fully return while keeping the connection to your Higher Self alive. You are now aligned, grounded, and deeply connected to your truest essence. Carry this feeling with you, knowing that you can return to this space of clarity and wisdom whenever you need it.

**Journaling Exercise**
Describe in vivid detail what your ideal, fully aligned life looks like. Close your eyes for a moment and picture it—

what do your days feel like? Where do you wake up, and how do you begin each morning? Is there a sense of peace, excitement, or deep fulfillment? Write as if you are already living it, fully immersed in the experience. Let the words flow without restriction.

Now, take a step back. What's stopping you from living this life right now? Maybe it's fear, self-doubt, or the belief that you're not ready. But what if you are? What if the only thing standing in your way is the idea that you have to wait for some perfect moment? Challenge that thought. Alignment isn't about waiting for the stars to align—it's about making choices today that reflect the person you want to be.

Think about small ways you can embody this version of yourself right now. If your ideal life includes creative freedom, can you carve out time to write, paint, or express yourself today? If it involves deep, meaningful relationships, how can you start nurturing those connections now? No action is too small. The more you step into this vision, the more natural it will feel.

As you write, notice any resistance. Do certain thoughts creep in—doubts, excuses, or the voice that says, this isn't possible for me? Acknowledge them, but don't let them define your truth. Rewrite those limiting beliefs into affirmations: I am worthy of this life. I am already stepping into it.

Let this exercise be a bridge between where you are and where you want to be. This isn't just an abstract dream—it's your reality, waiting for you to claim it. So, what does your aligned life look like? And more importantly, how can you start living it today?

# Building Spiritual Resilience

*"The strongest souls are not those who have never faced hardship, but those who have learned to rise, again and again, with faith and resilience."*

**What Is Spiritual Resilience**

Spiritual resilience is the quiet strength that keeps you standing when life's storms rage around you. It is not about avoiding hardship but about facing it with a sense of inner stability and trust. Life is unpredictable—there will be moments of loss, uncertainty, and struggle. But spiritual resilience is what allows you to navigate these moments without losing yourself in fear or despair.

At its core, resilience is about adaptability. It is not rigid strength but fluid strength—the ability to bend without breaking. Imagine a tree in a storm. The ones that survive are not the stiff, unyielding ones but the ones that sway, adjusting with the wind rather than resisting it. This same principle applies to spiritual resilience. The more you resist life's inevitable challenges, the more exhausting and painful they become. But when you cultivate resilience, you develop the capacity to remain present and centered, no matter what unfolds.

So, how do you strengthen this unshakable inner foundation? It begins with trust—trust in yourself, trust in the process, and trust in something greater than your immediate circumstances. Some call it faith, others call it surrender. It does not mean giving up control completely;

rather, it is about knowing when to hold on and when to let go.

Resilience is also built through consistent spiritual practices. Just as physical strength comes from repeated exercise, spiritual strength comes from small, intentional acts that reinforce your connection to yourself and the universe. Meditation, breathwork, affirmations, and acts of service all contribute to a more resilient spirit. The more you cultivate these practices in calm times, the more they will be there for you in difficult moments.

There will be times when you feel disconnected, when doubt creeps in, when fear whispers in your ear. That is okay. Resilience is not about never feeling lost—it is about always finding your way back. No setback is permanent, no wound is unhealable, and no storm lasts forever. The key is to build an unbreakable relationship with yourself, one that reminds you that even when everything around you feels uncertain, you are still whole.

**Daily Practices for Strengthening Spiritual Connection**
Spiritual resilience isn't built through grand gestures or occasional breakthroughs—it's woven into the fabric of your daily life through consistent, intentional practices. These small but powerful rituals serve as a foundation,

helping you remain steady and connected even when life feels uncertain. The key isn't perfection but presence. When you create moments throughout your day to realign, to breathe, to express gratitude, or to connect with something greater than yourself, you cultivate an inner strength that carries you through any challenge.

Mornings hold a special kind of magic. The way you begin your day shapes the energy you carry forward. Imagine waking up without immediately reaching for your phone or rushing into the day's demands. Instead, take a moment to ground yourself. This could be as simple as closing your eyes, inhaling deeply, and exhaling slowly, feeling the weight of your body as you wake up. You might whisper an intention: "I choose peace today." Some people light a candle, others place a hand on their heart and take a few mindful breaths. Even something as simple as sipping your morning tea or coffee with full awareness—feeling the warmth, noticing the aroma—can turn an ordinary act into a sacred ritual. These small acts remind you that each day is an opportunity to realign, to begin again with clarity and purpose.

Staying connected throughout the day doesn't require long, structured practices. It's about integrating simple moments of mindfulness into your routine. One of the most effective ways to stay grounded is through sensory awareness. The 5-4-3-2-1 method is an easy and powerful exercise to bring yourself back to the present moment: notice five things you see, four things you touch, three things you hear, two things you smell, and one thing you taste. This simple act shifts your focus from stress or worry to the immediate, tangible world around you. If you ever feel overwhelmed, try placing your bare feet on the ground, holding a small stone or crystal, or pressing your palm to your heart—these physical gestures send a signal to your mind that you are safe, present, and supported.

Gratitude is another essential practice for strengthening spiritual resilience. It shifts your focus from what's missing to what's already abundant in your life. Each night, before bed, take a moment to reflect on three things you're grateful for. These don't have to be grand or profound—"I heard my favorite song today," "The sunset was beautiful," or "I had a warm meal" are all simple acknowledgments that help rewire your mind toward positivity. The more you focus on the good, the more your perspective naturally shifts toward seeing blessings, even in difficult times.

For many, prayer or quiet reflection serves as a touchpoint of connection. This isn't about formal words or structured beliefs—it's about opening your heart, surrendering your fears, and finding comfort in something greater than yourself. It could be a spoken prayer, a whispered thought, or even a silent moment of communion with the universe. If traditional prayer doesn't resonate with you, consider repeating a mantra like "I am guided, I am protected, I am at peace." Even a brief moment of intentional stillness can bring a sense of calm and clarity.

Ultimately, spiritual resilience isn't about the length or complexity of your practices—it's about consistency and intention. Some days, all you might have time for is a single deep breath. Other days, you might sit in meditation, journal, or take a long walk in nature. The practice itself isn't what matters most—it's the commitment to showing up for yourself, even in the smallest ways. Each moment of presence strengthens your connection to your inner self, making it easier to navigate life's ups and downs with grace and resilience.

**Handling Negative Energy and Setbacks**

Negative energy and setbacks are an inevitable part of life, but they don't have to shake your foundation. The key to handling them isn't avoidance—it's learning how to remain centered despite them. Think of yourself as a tree.

When strong winds come, a tree doesn't resist; it bends, sways, and adapts, but its roots remain firmly planted in the ground. That's the goal here—not to eliminate negativity entirely, but to become so grounded in your own strength and truth that external chaos doesn't pull you out of alignment.

One of the first steps in dealing with negative energy is recognizing when it's not yours to carry. Have you ever walked into a room and suddenly felt drained or tense for no reason? Energy is contagious, and sometimes, we unconsciously absorb emotions from people around us. The best way to avoid this is by becoming aware of what belongs to you and what doesn't. If you're feeling heavy or anxious, take a moment to pause and ask yourself: Is this mine, or did I pick this up from someone else? If the energy isn't yours, visualize yourself releasing it—imagine it flowing out of your body like smoke, dissolving into the air.

When negativity comes in the form of external criticism or doubt, remind yourself that other people's opinions are reflections of their own beliefs, not your truth. Someone might project their fears onto you, telling you that your dreams are unrealistic or that change is impossible. Instead of internalizing their words, take a deep breath and remember: This is their story, not mine. You don't have to accept every thought or opinion that comes your way. Imagine yourself wearing a cloak of light that deflects negativity, allowing you to stay rooted in your own confidence and purpose.

Life challenges can also shake your sense of peace, whether it's an unexpected setback, a personal loss, or a period of uncertainty. In these moments, the natural reaction is often to resist, to wish things were different. But resistance creates suffering. Instead of fighting reality, practice surrender—not in the sense of giving up, but in trusting that even this moment has purpose. Ask yourself: What is this teaching me? Sometimes, the most painful experiences lead to the greatest growth.

When you feel overwhelmed, grounding techniques can help bring you back to center. Place your feet on the earth, take slow, deep breaths, or hold a grounding object like a stone or piece of wood. Visualize yourself as an unshakable mountain—strong, steady, and resilient, no matter what storms pass through. Another powerful tool is movement. Negative energy can get stuck in the body, so shake it out, go for a walk, dance, or do anything that physically resets your state.

Lastly, remember that setbacks are not the end of your journey—they are part of it. Think of any successful person or spiritual teacher; their strength didn't come from an easy path but from overcoming obstacles. Trust that every challenge is shaping you, refining you, and preparing you for something greater. You are not powerless in the face of negativity—you are stronger than you think.

**Guided Meditation**

Close your eyes and take a deep, intentional breath in through your nose. Feel the cool air filling your lungs, expanding your chest, and energizing every cell in your body. As you exhale, release any tension you might be holding—let go of the tightness in your shoulders, the weight in your chest, the clutter in your mind. With each breath, you sink deeper into stillness, allowing yourself to detach from the outside world and settle into the present moment.

Now, bring your awareness to your heart center. Imagine a soft light beginning to glow within you. This light is your inner peace, your unshakable core, the part of you that remains untouched by external circumstances. With each breath, the light grows stronger, expanding outward, filling your entire chest with warmth, safety, and serenity.

It spreads to your arms, your legs, the tips of your fingers, the top of your head—until your entire being is bathed in this radiant glow. This light is your foundation. No matter what happens outside of you, this peace remains.

Now, picture yourself standing in the middle of a vast, open field. The sky above is an endless blue, stretching infinitely in all directions. The sun shines warmly on your skin, and a gentle breeze moves through the grass. You are grounded, your feet planted firmly on the earth, deeply connected to its strength. Feel the solid ground beneath you, supporting you, reminding you that you are safe, steady, and strong.

Suddenly, a powerful wind begins to pick up around you. It howls, swirling dust and debris into the air. This wind represents the chaos of the world—the negativity, the stress, the doubts, and fears that try to shake your foundation. The wind pushes against you, but you do not move. You stand tall, like a mighty oak tree with deep roots. No matter how hard the wind blows, you remain grounded. You do not resist it. You do not fear it. You simply observe it, knowing that just like all things, it will pass.

Now, bring your attention inward once again. The golden light within you burns even brighter now, unwavering and strong. You realize that your peace does not come from outside circumstances—it comes from within. You are not at the mercy of the world; you are the stillness within the storm.

As you stand firm in this realization, repeat these affirmations in your mind:

*"I am calm and steady, no matter what happens around me."*

*"I am deeply rooted in my inner strength."*

*"I trust in my ability to navigate life's challenges with grace."*

*"I am the source of my own peace."*

Let these words settle into your being, anchoring you even deeper into a state of unshakable serenity. Imagine yourself walking through life with this same steadiness—no matter what arises, you remain centered, composed, and at peace.

Now, take another deep breath in, filling your body with this powerful sense of inner calm. As you exhale, feel yourself fully embracing this resilience. Slowly bring your awareness back to the present moment. Wiggle your fingers and toes, gently roll your shoulders, and when you are ready, open your eyes.

Carry this feeling with you. Let it be your shield against negativity, your anchor in difficult times, your reminder that no matter what happens, you are always in control of your inner world. The storms may come and go, but you—your peace, your strength, your spirit—remain unshaken.

**Journaling Exercise**
Take a deep breath and settle into the space where you feel most at ease. Open your journal and allow yourself to write freely, without judgment. This is your sacred space to explore, understand, and strengthen your spiritual resilience. Begin by reflecting on the areas of your life where you feel spiritually weak or disconnected. Are there moments when you doubt yourself? Times when external negativity easily influences your emotions? Situations where fear or uncertainty make you feel ungrounded?

Write about these experiences as honestly as you can. Describe the moments when your inner strength feels depleted. Is it when you're around certain people? When life takes an unexpected turn? When you feel overwhelmed by responsibilities? Try to pinpoint specific triggers. Do these moments come with physical sensations—tightness in the chest, a heavy feeling in the gut, or racing thoughts? Do they stem from past experiences, limiting beliefs, or patterns you've unconsciously carried?

Now, shift your focus to resilience. Imagine the strongest version of yourself—someone who remains steady, even in the face of adversity. What would it look like to navigate life with unwavering inner peace? Picture yourself handling challenges with grace, responding rather than reacting, and feeling a deep sense of trust in yourself and the universe. What habits, thoughts, or practices would help you cultivate this strength?

Write a list of intentions to build your spiritual resilience. Maybe you want to start a daily grounding practice, set stronger boundaries, or release attachment to things outside your control. Perhaps you need to trust your intuition more, practice self-compassion, or embrace change with an open heart. Be specific. If you feel drained by certain relationships, how can you protect your energy? If you struggle with self-doubt, what daily affirmations can help rewire your mindset? If stress weakens your connection to your higher self, how can you create more moments of stillness and presence?

As you write, allow yourself to feel empowered. Remind yourself that resilience isn't about being unaffected by life's difficulties; it's about learning how to move through them with strength, wisdom, and trust.

End your journaling session with an affirmation:

*"I am building resilience every day. No matter what challenges arise, I remain centered, strong, and deeply connected to my true self."*

Revisit this page whenever you need a reminder that your spiritual strength is always within reach. Let it be a space of encouragement, a reminder that you are always evolving, and that every challenge is an opportunity to deepen your connection with yourself and the divine.

# Sustaining Your Spiritual Detox Long-Term

*"Spiritual growth isn't a destination; it's a lifelong journey of realignment, renewal, and returning to yourself."*

**Making Spiritual Detox a Lifestyle**

Spiritual detox is not just a one-time reset; it's an ongoing practice, a commitment to yourself that evolves with time. Just as the body benefits from regular nourishment and movement, the spirit flourishes when given space to breathe, release, and realign. Making spiritual detox a lifestyle means creating a rhythm that naturally integrates these practices into your daily life—not as a rigid routine but as an intuitive, flowing process.

The first step in sustaining this long-term is self-awareness. Regularly checking in with yourself is essential. Ask: How am I feeling emotionally? What thoughts are dominating my mind? Is there tension in my body? These simple but powerful reflections help you recognize when something is off before it builds into a blockage. It's easy to get caught up in life's demands, but by setting aside even a few moments a day to pause and assess your internal state, you create the space needed for clarity and healing.

Clearing blockages as they arise prevents emotional and energetic stagnation. Sometimes, these blockages come from external sources—interactions, environments, or situations that drain your energy. Other times, they stem from within—unprocessed emotions, unresolved fears, or lingering self-doubt. When you notice something weighing on you, ask yourself: What is this feeling trying to tell me? Acknowledge it, but don't allow it to take root. Release can come in many forms—journaling, breathwork, movement, or simply giving yourself permission to feel and let go. The key is not to let these emotions settle in as permanent residents but rather to allow them to pass through you.

Staying aligned means consistently returning to what feels true for you. Life will always present distractions, external expectations, and pressures that attempt to pull you away from your center. But alignment is not about perfection—it's about returning to yourself again and again. Develop personal rituals that anchor you, whether that's a morning intention-setting practice, a gratitude reflection before bed, or moments of stillness throughout the day. These small, conscious choices keep you connected to your spiritual path without feeling forced or overwhelming.

True spiritual detox is not about avoiding challenges but learning to navigate them with greater ease and resilience. When practiced consistently, it becomes second nature—an internal compass guiding you back to balance, no matter where life takes you.

**Creating a Personalized Spiritual Routine**

There is no single right way to maintain spiritual detox—it's all about what works for you. Your spiritual routine should feel like a natural extension of your life, not a set of obligations you force yourself to complete. It's not about perfection, nor is it about checking off a list of spiritual practices just because they seem "good" for you. Instead, it's about building a rhythm that keeps you grounded, aligned, and connected to your higher self.

Daily practices form the foundation of your spiritual routine, the non-negotiables that keep your energy clear and your mind centered. They don't have to be grand gestures or time-consuming rituals. Sometimes, the simplest things have the biggest impact. Waking up and taking three deep breaths before looking at your phone can shift your entire day. Setting an intention before stepping into a meeting or sending an email can change the way you communicate. Drinking water with mindfulness, feeling the nourishment in every sip, can be a detoxifying practice in itself.

Some people thrive on structured daily rituals—morning meditation, yoga, journaling, breathwork. If that feels right for you, fantastic. Others need flexibility, weaving mindfulness into the flow of their day rather than setting aside rigid blocks of time. Maybe you take a deep breath every time you touch a doorknob, using that moment as a reminder to center yourself. Perhaps you listen to calming frequencies while working or practice gratitude before each meal. The key is finding what effortlessly integrates into your life, making spirituality a natural and consistent part of your day.

Weekly practices take the spiritual detox a step further, offering deeper restoration and reflection. These might include longer meditation sessions, an energy-clearing ritual, or dedicating an hour to journaling about your emotions, progress, and blockages. You might take a nature walk every Sunday to reset, allowing the elements to refresh your mind and body. A weekly digital detox—perhaps a full day without social media or external distractions—can be a game-changer for mental clarity. Some people like to do a "Sunday reset," where they cleanse their space, light candles or incense, and reflect on their week. Others find connection in attending a spiritual gathering, whether that's a religious service, a sound bath, or a simple tea ritual with like-minded souls.

Monthly practices are about big-picture alignment. They offer an opportunity to zoom out and reassess: Are you in tune with your soul's desires? Are there emotional or energetic blockages you need to release? Monthly practices can be more intensive, such as a deep house cleansing with smudging and sound healing, a solo retreat for introspection, or a detailed tarot or oracle reading to check in with your spiritual path. Some people follow lunar cycles, using the new moon for setting intentions and the full moon for releasing what no longer serves them. Others find power in fasting, either physically or energetically, as a way to clear out old energy and invite in new clarity.

One of the most powerful things you can do is create a spiritual "check-in" ritual each month. Sit down with your journal, light a candle, and ask yourself:

How have I been feeling lately?

*What is draining me?*

*What is nourishing me?*

*What am I resisting, and why?*

*What steps can I take to realign with my highest self?*

By making space for honest reflection, you avoid slipping into old patterns and ensure that your spiritual detox remains an ongoing, evolving journey.

The beauty of a personalized spiritual routine is that it grows with you. Some seasons of life will call for more stillness and introspection, while others will require movement and action. Your routine isn't meant to be a strict set of rules—it's a dynamic, living practice that shifts with your needs. The real question isn't, "What should I be doing?" but rather, "What makes me feel alive, connected, and at peace?"

Listen to that answer, and build your routine around it. Let it be your guide.

**Recognizing When You Need Another Detox**
Recognizing when you need another detox is an art—one that requires self-awareness, honesty, and a willingness to pause before burnout sets in. The truth is, no matter how much inner work you do, life will always bring new challenges, emotions, and energies that need processing. Spiritual detox isn't about achieving a permanent state of clarity; it's about continuously maintaining and realigning your inner world as you grow.

So, how do you know when it's time for another reset? The signs aren't always obvious, but they are persistent.

Maybe you're feeling ungrounded—like your mind is constantly racing, and no matter how much you try to focus, you can't seem to center yourself. Meditation feels forced, journaling no longer brings clarity, and your intuition, which once felt like a trusted guide, now seems distant. It's as if you're floating through your days rather than moving with intention.

Or perhaps your emotions feel heavier than usual. You snap at people over small things, or you find yourself withdrawing from social situations that once brought you joy. You're more reactive, more irritable, and there's a lingering exhaustion that sleep doesn't seem to fix. Even the things that usually bring you peace—reading, nature, solitude—feel dull or ineffective.

Another sign? The creeping return of old patterns. The habits you thought you'd outgrown suddenly make their way back into your life. You start scrolling mindlessly on social media, comparing yourself to others, falling into self-doubt, or numbing yourself with distractions. The clarity you once had about your purpose and direction starts to feel murky again.

And then there's the energy drain. Certain spaces and people feel heavier than before. Interactions that used to be neutral now leave you exhausted, and you start avoiding deep conversations because you don't have the emotional bandwidth for them. If you find yourself dreading commitments, over-explaining yourself, or constantly feeling like you need to "perform" for others, it's a sign that external energies are seeping into your inner space.

The question is: *What do you do when you recognize these signs?*

First, let go of the idea that needing another detox means you've failed. There's no such thing as a one-time cleanse that keeps your energy clear forever. Just as your body needs regular nourishment and rest, your spirit requires regular detoxification and alignment. Every season of life brings new lessons, challenges, and experiences that shape and shift your energy. The fact that you're aware of your need for a reset means you're evolving.

Second, embrace the ebb and flow of your spiritual journey. Imagine your spiritual well-being like the ocean—sometimes calm, sometimes turbulent, but always in motion. Instead of resisting the waves, learn to move with them. When you feel the buildup of emotional or energetic weight, don't ignore it. See it as a natural part of your cycle, a sign that you're ready for deeper clarity.

So, how do you approach your next detox?

It doesn't always have to be drastic. Sometimes, a full reset is needed—a weekend of solitude, deep cleansing rituals, or a conscious unplugging from external noise. Other times, a soft reset is enough—taking a step back, creating quiet space in your day, or simply giving yourself permission to rest. The key is to listen to what your spirit needs.

You might start with something simple:

A full day without social media to clear your mind.

A deep journaling session to release any suppressed emotions.

Spending time in nature, barefoot on the earth, reconnecting with its grounding energy.

A ritual bath with salt and essential oils to cleanse stagnant energy.

A guided meditation focused on releasing what no longer serves you.

The most important thing? Approach your detox with love, not guilt.

Too often, we resist taking a step back because we think we "should" have everything figured out by now. But growth isn't linear. There will always be moments when you need to recalibrate, to pause and realign before moving forward. Instead of seeing it as a setback, see it as a sacred act of self-care.

Think of it this way: Every detox you go through strengthens your ability to navigate life with more ease and awareness. Each reset deepens your connection to yourself, making it easier to recognize when you're out of alignment and what you need to regain balance. Over time, these detoxes become second nature—less about "fixing" yourself and more about maintaining a state of clarity and flow.

So, if you're feeling disconnected, overwhelmed, or just off, take it as a sign, not a failure. You're not going backward—you're simply evolving into the next version of yourself. Honor that.

When your soul whispers for a reset, listen.

It's not an ending. It's a new beginning.

**Guided Meditation**

Sit comfortably, either cross-legged on the floor or in a chair with your feet flat on the ground. Let your hands rest gently on your lap, palms facing up. Close your eyes and take a deep breath in through your nose, filling your lungs completely. Hold for a moment. Then, exhale slowly through your mouth, releasing any tension.

With each breath, let your body relax. Feel the weight of your shoulders drop, the muscles in your face soften, and any lingering stress dissolve. Allow your breath to find its natural rhythm—steady, calm, and effortless.

Now, bring your awareness inward. Imagine yourself sitting at the edge of a quiet river. The water is clear and smooth, gently flowing past you. With each inhale, the water absorbs any tension, washing it away as it drifts downstream. Each exhale releases heaviness, allowing the current to carry it far beyond your reach. The more you breathe, the more you become one with the steady, calming rhythm of the river.

As you focus on this peaceful sound, allow it to expand with each inhale. It grows steadier, lighter, filling your entire chest, spreading through your arms, down your spine, into your legs, until your entire being is bathed in this radiant energy. This peace is your connection to the divine, to the universe, to your highest self.

Now, visualize your day unfolding before you. See yourself waking up in the morning, feeling clear, energized, and centered. You begin the day with an intention—perhaps gratitude, self-love, or mindfulness. Notice how setting this intention gently guides your thoughts and actions.

As you move through the day, picture yourself engaging in small spiritual practices. Maybe it's a few moments of stillness with your morning tea, a mindful breath before answering an email, or silently sending love to a stranger on the street. These small moments anchor you, reminding you that spirituality isn't separate from life—it is woven into every moment.

Now, envision a challenge arising—a difficult conversation, a moment of doubt, an unexpected stressor. Instead of reacting with tension, see yourself pausing. You take a breath, place a hand on your heart, and reconnect with the golden light inside you. You remember that you are grounded, supported, and in control of how you respond. With this awareness, you navigate the situation with grace and clarity.

Continue watching your day unfold with this deep sense of connection. See yourself moving through it with ease, integrating your spiritual practices effortlessly, feeling aligned with your highest self.

As this visualization comes to a close, bring your attention back to your breath. Feel the support of the ground beneath you. Slowly, begin to wiggle your fingers and toes, bringing movement back into your body. When you're ready, open your eyes.

Take a moment to absorb this energy. Know that this connection is always within you. No matter how busy life gets, no matter what challenges arise, you can always return to this steadiness.

You are whole. You are aligned. You are deeply connected to the sacred in every moment.

**Journaling Exercise**
Think of this as designing a long-term spiritual blueprint—something that will guide you but also grow and change with you. Begin by setting the tone for your journaling session. Light a candle, play some calming music, or sit in a space that makes you feel relaxed and connected. Then, ask yourself: What does spiritual well-being truly mean to me? Is it about feeling more peaceful? More present? More aligned with my purpose? Write freely, without worrying about structure. Let your intuition lead the way.

Now, reflect on what has brought you the most clarity, peace, and growth in your spiritual detox journey so far. Maybe you've noticed that starting the day with breathwork keeps you grounded, or perhaps journaling has helped you untangle emotions that once felt overwhelming. Write about these moments in detail. Describe how they felt, what shifted in you, and why they mattered. These are the practices worth keeping.

Next, gently explore the areas where you struggle. Are there days when you abandon your spiritual practices? What tends to throw you off track—stress, exhaustion, distractions? Be honest, but approach this with self-compassion. You're not looking for flaws to fix; you're simply identifying patterns that could use more care and attention.

Now, start crafting your personalized spiritual maintenance plan. Imagine your ideal daily routine—not the one that feels forced or unrealistic, but one that genuinely excites and supports you. Maybe it's waking up and spending five minutes in stillness before reaching for your phone, or dedicating one evening a week to a deeper practice like breathwork or energy cleansing. Let it be flexible.

Think about your weekly and monthly rituals, too. What could you do at the start of each new week to reset your energy? Perhaps a digital detox for a few hours, a grounding ritual, or writing down intentions for the days ahead. On a monthly level, maybe you want to do a more in-depth check-in, reflecting on what's been working and what needs adjusting. You could even plan small spiritual retreats—whether that means a quiet weekend for yourself, a nature getaway, or attending a workshop that inspires you.

As you write, allow yourself to dream. What would it feel like to live in total alignment with your spiritual needs? Describe it in vivid detail. Picture yourself waking up, moving through your day, handling challenges with grace, and ending each night with a sense of fulfillment. Now, ask yourself: What small steps can I take today to start embodying that vision?

This plan isn't about perfection. It's a living, breathing guide that you can revisit, adjust, and reshape as you grow. Keep it somewhere visible, return to it often, and most importantly—allow it to serve you, rather than feeling like something you have to serve.

# A New Beginning

*"Growth is not about reaching a final destination—it is about continuously returning to yourself, again and again, with deeper wisdom and greater love."*

As you reach this point in your journey, take a moment to pause and truly recognize the transformation you have undergone. It's easy to keep striving for the next milestone, the next breakthrough, or the next moment of clarity, but before you move forward, look back. Think about who you were when you first started this journey. Recall the thoughts, emotions, and struggles that brought you here. You have done deep, often challenging inner work, uncovering layers of yourself that were once hidden or ignored. That alone is something to celebrate.

Growth is not always obvious while you're in the middle of it. Much like how a seed grows beneath the soil before breaking through the surface, much of your spiritual and emotional progress may have happened quietly, without immediate visible results. But make no mistake—change has occurred. You have released burdens, redefined beliefs, and reconnected with parts of yourself that had been neglected. Perhaps your emotions feel lighter, your thoughts clearer, and your connection to your inner self stronger. Or maybe the shifts have been more subtle—small but powerful moments of peace, deeper self-awareness, or a renewed sense of purpose.

Acknowledging this transformation is essential because the mind often dismisses progress in favor of what still needs improvement. But spiritual growth is not about reaching a final destination; it's about evolving continuously, deepening your understanding, and staying aligned with your truth. Consider how you now respond to challenges differently, how your inner dialogue has shifted, or how you've created space for more love, peace, and clarity in your life.

Take a deep breath and allow yourself to appreciate the work you have done. This is not the end of your journey— it is a new beginning, a foundation upon which you will continue to build. The practices you have explored are not meant to be a temporary fix but a lifelong commitment to self-awareness, healing, and alignment. You have equipped yourself with the tools to navigate life with greater resilience, authenticity, and purpose.

Now, as you reflect on all that you have uncovered, consider what you want to carry forward. What lessons will stay with you? What practices have become essential to your well-being? What beliefs no longer serve you? This is your opportunity to consciously step into the next phase of your life with intention, clarity, and confidence.

Just as the body requires continuous nourishment and care, so does the spirit. There will be moments when you feel completely aligned, full of energy and clarity, and others when life's challenges make you feel disconnected or weighed down again. That's not a failure; it's simply part of the cycle.

You are not meant to be in a constant state of perfection or enlightenment. True spiritual resilience comes from knowing how to realign yourself whenever you feel off balance. Think of everything you have learned and practiced throughout this journey—not as rigid rules to follow, but as tools that will always be there when you need them. When you start feeling emotionally drained, mentally foggy, or spiritually lost, you now have the awareness to recognize it and the ability to gently guide yourself back.

This is what makes spiritual detox an ongoing evolution. It's not about avoiding challenges but about approaching them with a different mindset. Instead of fearing setbacks, you now see them as opportunities for deeper self-reflection. Instead of letting negativity consume you, you know how to cleanse and protect your energy. Instead of feeling trapped by limiting beliefs, you've gained the power to break free and move forward with confidence.

Every step you take on this path will reveal something new. As you grow, your needs will shift, your perspectives will expand, and your connection with yourself will deepen. Some of the practices that resonate with you now may evolve over time, while others will remain foundational. That's the beauty of this journey—it is uniquely yours, and you are always in control of how you navigate it.

Embracing this as a lifelong commitment doesn't mean constantly working on yourself or always striving for more. It means cultivating self-awareness, practicing self-compassion, and honoring your needs as they arise. It means allowing yourself the grace to pause, the courage to keep going, and the wisdom to trust that you are always exactly where you need to be.

Your spiritual detox is not ending here. It is becoming a way of life—one that will continue to unfold, shape you, and lead you toward deeper peace, authenticity, and fulfillment.

No matter where you are right now, know that you are capable of sustaining this journey. You have already taken the most important step—the willingness to grow, to let go, and to align with your true self. That courage alone is proof of your strength.

There will be days when you feel deeply connected, as if everything is flowing effortlessly. There will also be days when doubt creeps in, when old habits resurface, when life feels heavy again. That's okay. Healing and growth are not linear. The key is to remember that every moment is an opportunity to begin again. There is no failure, only learning. No setbacks, only invitations to deepen your awareness.

Trust yourself. Trust your intuition. You already have everything you need within you. The practices, rituals, and insights you've embraced throughout this journey are not just temporary tools—they are lifelines that will always be there when you need them.

When the world feels overwhelming, return to your breath. When negativity surrounds you, cleanse your space and protect your energy. When fear and doubt arise, reconnect with your higher self and remind yourself of your truth. When you feel lost, journal your thoughts, reflect on your journey, and remember how far you've come.

You are never alone on this path. The universe supports you. Your own soul guides you. And you now have the wisdom to keep moving forward, even when the road feels uncertain.

Made in the USA
Monee, IL
11 April 2025